THE
CALL

COUNTING THE COST
OF FOLLOWING CHRIST

LifeWay Press®
Nashville, Tennessee

DISCIPLES PATH

Disciples Path is a series of studies founded on Jesus' model of discipleship. Created by experienced disciple makers across the nation, it offers an intentional pathway for transformational discipleship and a way to help followers of Christ move from new disciples to mature disciple makers. Each study in the series is built on the principles of modeling, practicing, and multiplying:

- Leaders model the life of a biblical disciple.

- Disciples follow and practice from the leader.

- Disciples become disciple makers and multiply through the *Disciples Path*.

Each study in the series has been written and approved by disciple makers for small groups and one-on-one settings.

Contributor:

Dr. Craig Etheredge; First Baptist Church; Colleyville, Texas

MINISTRY GRID
training made simple

For helps on how to use *Disciples Path,* tips on how to better lead groups, or additional ideas for leading this study, visit ministrygrid.com/web/disciplespath.

© 2015 LifeWay Press® • Reprinted 2018

ISBN 978-1-4300-3952-5 • Item 005717352

Dewey decimal classification: 248.84
Subject headings: GOD—WILL \ DISCIPLESHIP \ CHRISTIAN LIFE

Eric Geiger
Vice President, LifeWay Resources

Rick Howerton
Discipleship Specialist

Sam O'Neal, Joel Polk
Content Editors

Brian Daniel
Manager, Discipleship Publishing

Michael Kelley
Director, Groups Ministry

We believe that the Bible has God for its author; salvation for its end; and truth, without any mixture of error, for its matter and that all Scripture is totally true and trustworthy. To review LifeWay's doctrinal guideline, visit lifeway.com/doctrinalguideline.

To order additional copies of this resource, write to LifeWay Resources Customer Service; One LifeWay Plaza; Nashville, TN 37234; fax 615-251-5933; call toll free 800-458-2772; order online at LifeWay.com; email orderentry@lifeway.com; or visit the LifeWay Christian Store serving you.

Printed in the United States of America

Groups Ministry Publishing • LifeWay Resources
One LifeWay Plaza • Nashville, TN 37234

CONTENTS

A NOTE FOR DISCIPLE MAKERS

Several years ago I was part of a massive research study that sought to discover how the Lord often brings about transformation in the hearts of His people. The study became a book called *Transformational Discipleship*. Basically, we wanted to learn how disciples are made. Based on the study of Scripture and lots of interactions with people, we concluded that transformation is likely to occur when a godly **leader** applies **truth** to the heart of a person while that person is in a teachable **posture.**

- **LEADER:** You are the leader. As you invest in the people you're discipling, they will learn much about the Christian faith by watching you, by sensing your heart for the Lord, and by seeing you pursue Him. I encourage you to seek to be the type of leader who can say, "Follow my example as I follow the example of Christ."

- **TRUTH:** All six studies in the *Disciples Path* series were developed in deep collaboration with ministry leaders who regularly and effectively disciple people. The studies are designed to take the people you disciple into the Word of God—because we're confident that Jesus and His Word sanctify us and transform us. Our community of disciple makers mapped out a path of the truths we believe are essential for each believer to know and understand.

- **POSTURE:** Hopefully the people you will be investing in adopt a teachable posture—one that is open and hungry for the Lord. Encourage them to take the study seriously and to view your invitation to study together as a sacred opportunity to experience the grace of God and the truth of God.

We hope and pray the Lord will use this study in your life and the lives of those you disciple. As you apply the truth of God to teachable hearts, transformation will occur. Thank you for being a disciple maker!

In Christ,

Eric

Eric Geiger
Vice President, LifeWay Christian Resources
Coauthor of *Transformational Discipleship*

WHAT IS A DISCIPLE?

Congratulations! If you've chosen to live as a disciple of Jesus, you've made the most important decision imaginable. But you may be wondering, *What does it mean to be a disciple?*

To put it simply, a disciple of Jesus is someone who has chosen to follow Jesus. That's the command Jesus gave to those He recruited as His first disciples: "Follow Me." In Jesus' culture, religious leaders called rabbis would gather a group of followers called disciples to follow in their footsteps and learn their teachings. In the same way, you will become more and more like Jesus as you purposefully follow Him in the weeks to come. Jesus once said, "Everyone who is fully trained will be like his teacher" (Luke 6:40).

On a deeper level, disciples of Jesus are those learning to base their identities on Jesus Himself. All of us use different labels to describe who we are at the core levels of our hearts. Some think of themselves as athletes or intellectuals. Others think of themselves as professionals, parents, leaders, class clowns, and so on.

Disciples of Jesus set aside those labels and base their identities on Him. For example:

- **A disciple of Jesus is a child of God.** In the Bible we find these words: "Look at how great a love the Father has given us that we should be called God's children. And we are!" (1 John 3:1). We are God's children. He loves us as our perfect Father.

- **A disciple of Jesus is an alien in this world.** Disciples of Jesus are aliens, or outsiders, in their own cultures. Because of this identity, Jesus' disciples abstain from actions and activities that are contrary to Him. Peter, one of Jesus' original disciples, wrote these words: "Dear friends, I urge you as strangers and temporary residents to abstain from fleshly desires that war against you" (1 Pet. 2:11).

- **A disciple of Jesus is an ambassador for Christ.** Another of Jesus' disciples recorded these words in the Bible: "Therefore, if anyone is in Christ, he is a new creation; old things have passed away, and look, new things have come. Therefore, we are ambassadors for Christ, certain that God is appealing through us. We plead on Christ's behalf, 'Be reconciled to God'" (2 Cor. 5:17,20). Ambassadors represent their king and country in a different culture for a specified period of time. Because we have been transformed by Jesus and are now His disciples and ambassadors, we represent Him to the world through our actions and by telling others about Him.

The journey you are about to take is one that will transform you more and more to be like Jesus. Enjoy! No one ever loved and cared for people more passionately than Jesus. No one was ever more sincere in His concern for others than Jesus. And no one ever gave more so that we could experience His love than Jesus did on the cross.

As you grow to be more like Jesus, you'll find that your relationships are stronger, you have more inner peace than ever before, and you look forward to the future as never before.

That's the blessing of living as a disciple of Jesus.

HOW TO USE THIS RESOURCE

Welcome to *The Call*. By exploring the journey of Jesus' earliest disciples, both new and established Christians will gain a better understanding of what it means to follow Christ. As you get started, consider the following guides and suggestions for making the most of this experience.

GROUP DISCUSSION

Because the process of discipleship always involves at least two people—the leader and the disciple—each session of *The Call* includes a practical plan for group engagement and discussion.

This plan includes the following steps:

- **GET STARTED.** The first section of the group material helps you ease into the discussion by starting on common ground. You'll begin by reflecting on the previous session and your recent experiences as a disciple. After spending time in prayer, you'll find a practical illustration to help you launch into the main topic of the current session.

- **THE STORY.** While using *Disciples Path*, you'll find opportunities to engage the Bible through both story and teaching. That's why the group time for each session features two main sections: **Know the Story** and **Unpack the Story. Know the Story** introduces a biblical text and includes follow-up questions for brief discussion. It's recommended that your group encounter the biblical text by reading it out loud. **Unpack the Story** includes practical teaching material and discussion questions—both designed to help you engage the truths contained in the biblical text. To make the most of your experience, use the provided material as a launching point for deeper conversation. As you read through the teaching material and engage the questions as a group, be thinking of how the truths you're exploring will impact your everyday life.

- **ENGAGE.** The group portion of each session ends with an activity designed to help you practice the biblical principles introduced in **Know the Story** and more fully explored in **Unpack the Story.** This part of the group time often appeals to different learning styles and will push you to engage the text at a personal level.

INDIVIDUAL DISCOVERY

Each session of *The Call* also includes content for individual use during the time between group gatherings. This content is divided into three categories:

↑ **Worship:** features content for worship and devotion. These activities provide opportunities for you to connect with God in meaningful ways and deepen your relationship with Him.

➡ ⬅ **Personal study:** features content for personal study. These pages help you gain a deeper understanding of the truths and principles explored during the group discussion.

⬅ ➡ **Application:** features content for practical application. These suggestions help you take action based on the information you've learned and your encounters with God.

Note: Aside from the **Reading Plan,** the content provided in the Individual Discovery portion of each session should be considered optional. You'll get the most out of your personal study by working with your group leader to create a personalized discipleship plan using the **Weekly Activities** checklist included in each session.

ADDITIONAL SUGGESTIONS

- You'll be best prepared for each group discussion or mentoring conversation if you read the session material beforehand. A serious read will serve you most effectively, but skimming the **Get Started** and **The Story** sections will also be helpful if time is limited.

- The deeper you're willing to engage in the group discussions and individual discovery each session, the more you'll benefit from those experiences. Don't hold back, and don't be afraid to ask questions whenever necessary.

- As you explore the **Engage** portion of each session, you'll have the chance to practice different activities and spiritual disciplines. Take advantage of the chance to observe others during the group time—and to ask questions—so that you'll be prepared to incorporate these activities into your private spiritual life as well.

- Visit lifeway.com/disciplespath for a free PDF download that includes leader helps for *The Call* and additional resources for disciple makers.

WHO IS JESUS?

Jesus is worth following because
there is no one like Him.

REFLECT

Welcome to *The Call*. The goal of this resource is to help you explore the process of growing and maturing as a disciple of Jesus. Throughout the following sessions, we'll examine the identity of Jesus as well as the identity and characteristics of a true disciple. In this session, we'll begin by gaining a better understanding of who Jesus is and why we should choose to follow Him.

What have you learned about Jesus over the course of your life?

Who do people say Jesus is today?

PRAY

Take a break from your discussion to approach God in prayer. Use the following guidelines as you connect with Him:

- Thank God for the opportunity to join with other disciples of Christ in order to gain a better understanding of who Jesus is.

- Praise God for the ways He has worked in your life and the things He has done.

- Ask for an open mind and heart to best see what He wants to reveal to you today.

INTRODUCTION

Jesus Christ. Most people have heard of Him. Most people have an opinion of Him. If you're looking for excitement, try going to a public area and asking people, "Who is Jesus?" You'll likely get a variety of answers and reactions.

The fact is, no one else has changed history and affected our culture more than Jesus. More books have been written about Him, more music composed for Him, more art reflecting Him, more architecture and buildings designed for Him, and more organizations and foundations created in His name than for any other person.

He changed history. In the name of Jesus, hospitals and orphanages have been built, the care for the elderly and homeless have been emphasized, and organizations for the hungry and needy have been created. Churches have been established in His name on every continent in the world. All this for a Man who never wrote a book, never attended a university, never ran for office, never led a company, and lived 2,000 years ago.

The question remains, who is Jesus?

Was He simply a Jewish carpenter turned preacher? Was He a political zealot? Was He a false teacher who deceived the people? Was He a misguided miracle worker? Was He a lunatic with a death wish? Was He a spiritual guru or teacher? Was He one among many or was He one of a kind? At the end of the day, everyone must answer the question, "Who is Jesus?"

In this session we're going to look at the uniqueness of Jesus. We are going to see what makes Him stand head and shoulders above the rest, and why He is worth following with all of your heart.

What is your reaction to the statement "At the end of the day, everyone must answer the question 'Who is Jesus?' "

KNOW THE STORY

According to tradition, Jesus was 30 years old and living in Nazareth when He left His work as a craftsman and began His ministry. From this point forward, Jesus began to reveal His identity to a handful of men who would later turn the world upside down.

[35] Again the next day, John was standing with two of his disciples. [36] When he saw Jesus passing by, he said, "Look! The Lamb of God!" [37] The two disciples heard him say this and followed Jesus. [38] When Jesus turned and noticed them following Him, He asked them, "What are you looking for?" They said to Him, " Rabbi" (which means "Teacher"), "where are You staying?" [39] "Come and you'll see," He replied. So they went and saw where He was staying, and they stayed with Him that day. It was about 10 in the morning. [40] Andrew, Simon Peter's brother, was one of the two who heard John and followed Him. [41] He first found his own brother Simon and told him, "We have found the Messiah!" (which means "Anointed One"), [42] and he brought Simon to Jesus. When Jesus saw him, He said, "You are Simon, son of John. You will be called Cephas" (which means "Rock"). [43] The next day He decided to leave for Galilee. Jesus found Philip and told him, "Follow Me!" [44] Now Philip was from Bethsaida, the hometown of Andrew and Peter. [45] Philip found Nathanael and told him, "We have found the One Moses wrote about in the Law (and so did the prophets): Jesus the son of Joseph, from Nazareth!" [46] "Can anything good come out of Nazareth?" Nathanael asked him. "Come and see," Philip answered. [47] Then Jesus saw Nathanael coming toward Him and said about him, "Here is a true Israelite; no deceit is in him." [48] "How do you know me?" Nathanael asked. "Before Philip called you, when you were under the fig tree, I saw you," Jesus answered. [49] "Rabbi," Nathanael replied, "You are the Son of God! You are the King of Israel!" [50] Jesus responded to him, "Do you believe only because I told you I saw you under the fig tree? You will see greater things than this." [51] Then He said, "I assure you: You will see heaven opened and the angels of God ascending and descending on the Son of Man."

JOHN 1:35-51

Notice all of the different names (or titles) given to Jesus. Why do you think there are so many?

Notice the two times the phrase "Come and see" is used. What are people being invited to see?

UNPACK THE STORY

SON OF MAN

In this story, Jesus begins to reveal His identity to a few men. Each name or title for Jesus unveils an aspect of His identity as the God-Man.

Several of the titles attributed to Jesus in the first chapter of the Gospel of John reflect His humanity. "Rabbi" was a term of respect given to a spiritual teacher (see John 1:38). "Lamb of God" referred to His physical death on the cross as a substitute for our sin (see John 1:36). But the phrase "Son of Man" was special (see John 1:51)—it was Jesus' favorite way to refer to Himself. In fact, the Hebrew term is found 81 times in the New Testament Gospels, 30 of those in the Book of Matthew alone.

Why is it important to understand Jesus' humanity?

Jesus was a human, just like you and me. He wasn't a mythical person. He wasn't a legend. He wasn't an illusion that only appeared to be human. Jesus was a real, historical person.

The phrase "Son of Man" was a reference to His humanity. By using this term, He was declaring Himself to be a part of mankind. Jesus was a human, just like you and me. He wasn't a mythical person. He wasn't a legend. He wasn't an illusion that only appeared to be human. Jesus was a real, historical person. Hebrews 2:17 says that Jesus "had to be like His brothers in every way" so that He could help us in our time of need. John, one of Jesus' disciples, spoke of Jesus this way:

> We proclaim to you the one who existed from the beginning, whom we have heard and seen. We saw him with our own eyes and touched him with our own hands. He is the Word of life.
> **1 JOHN 1:1 (NLT)**

John was saying, "We have heard Jesus, we have seen Him with our eyes, we have touched Him with our hands!" Jesus was fully human.

What questions or observations do you have about Jesus' humanity?

SON OF GOD

Another title given to Jesus was "Son of God." Nathanael declared, "You are the Son of God! You are the King of Israel!" (John 1:49). This term is a clear statement of Jesus' divine nature. While Jesus claimed to be fully human like you and me, He also claimed to be fully God, which is not like anyone else in human history.

Read the following conclusions from eyewitnesses to all that Jesus said and did.

- Peter—Acts 2:29-36
- John the Baptist—John 3:25-36
- John the apostle—1 John 5:11-13
- Thomas—John 20:24-28

What are your observations from these passages?

What did the people closest to Jesus conclude about His identity?

Jesus wasn't just another moral teacher or spiritual leader. He was much more than that. Other religious leaders point to the way, but Jesus declared, "I am the way." Others claim to have some knowledge of truth, but Jesus said, "I am the truth." Others point to a path for living, but Jesus said, "I am the life" (see John 14:6). His claims set Him apart from everyone else.

Jesus claimed to be the "Son of Man"—fully human and the fulfillment of the promised Messiah. He also claimed to be the "Son of God"—God in the flesh who created the world, has authority over all things, and is coming again to judge and to rule. Ultimately Jesus backed up these claims by raising from the dead and showing Himself to be alive. The claims of Jesus are clear. But the response to His claims is a choice every person must ultimately make.

Was Jesus crazy when He made these claims? Was Jesus lying to the people around Him? Or was He who He actually claimed to be? One thing is sure, Jesus didn't leave us the option of labeling Him a good moral teacher. A good moral teacher doesn't claim to be God—unless it's true.

Jesus didn't leave us the option of labeling Him a good moral teacher. A good moral teacher doesn't claim to be God— unless it's true.

ENGAGE

Jesus is worth following because no one is like Him. He is completely unique. He stands in a class all His own. When we were far from God, estranged from Him and chasing our own way, Jesus came to us. But His coming wasn't celebrated with worship and obedience. His own people rejected Him. Yet to those who receive Him, to those who acknowledge Him and worship Him, He gives life. Consider how Paul states this in Philippians 2:5-11:

> [5] Make your own attitude that of Christ Jesus, [6] who, existing in the form of God, did not consider equality with God as something to be used for His own advantage. [7] Instead He emptied Himself by assuming the form of a slave, taking on the likeness of men. And when He had come as a man in His external form, [8] He humbled Himself by becoming obedient to the point of death—even to death on a cross. [9] For this reason God highly exalted Him and gave Him the name that is above every name, [10] so that at the name of Jesus every knee will bow—of those who are in heaven and on earth and under the earth— [11] and every tongue should confess that Jesus Christ is Lord, to the glory of God the Father.
>
> **PHILIPPIANS 2:5-11**

Why did Jesus become a man according to Philippians 2:5-11?

For those of you who can or would like to, take this opportunity to get on your knees for prayer. As you pray, acknowledge Jesus for who He is and what He has done. Commit your life to obeying and following Him. Pray for one another, that as a group you will worship and follow Him closely this week.

PRAYER REQUESTS

....

....

....

....

....

....

....

In addition to studying God's Word, work with your group leader to create a plan for personal study, worship, and application between now and the next session. Select from the following optional activities to match your personal preferences and available time.

⬆ Worship

☑ Read your Bible. Complete the reading plan on page 16.

☐ Connect with God by engaging the devotional on page 17.

☐ Read Philippians 2:5-11 again. The conclusion of this passage states, "At the name of Jesus every knee will bow—of those who are in heaven and on earth and under the earth—and every tongue should confess that Jesus Christ is Lord." Begin each morning this week kneeling before Jesus. Worship and praise Him for who He is and what He has done in your life.

➡⬅ Personal Study

☐ Read and interact with "Jesus: Fully Human" on page 18.

☐ Read and interact with "Jesus: Fully God" on page 20.

⬅➡ Application

☐ Share with others. Take the time to share something you have learned this week. Maybe you can start at home with your family. Or maybe you know someone at work or in your neighborhood who has spiritual questions. You may also want to share your favorite verse with friends through social media.

☐ Memorize John 14:6: "Jesus told him, 'I am the way, the truth, and the life. No one comes to the Father except through Me.'"

☐ Start a journal. Select one of the following passages and read it slowly several times. Consider what it's telling you about Jesus. Write down your thoughts and observations: John 1:1-14; 14:1-6; Colossians 1:15-20; Hebrews 1:1-4.

☐ Other:

WORSHIP

READING PLAN

Read through the following Scripture passages this week. Use the space provided to record your thoughts and responses.

Day 1
Isaiah 9:1-7

Day 2
Isaiah 44:6-23

Day 3
John 6:22-33

Day 4
John 6:34-59

Day 5
John 8:12-29

Day 6
Romans 8:31-39

Day 7
Hebrews 2:5-18

WHO DO YOU SAY HE IS?

Before people can come to know Christ personally, they have to "come and see" who Jesus is. They have to do their own investigation. How did the prophecies of the Messiah point to Jesus? What does the evidence say about Jesus? Who did Jesus claim to be? What did others say about Jesus' identity?

Look at some of the following prophecies about the coming Messiah and how they were fulfilled in the life of Jesus. (Note: These prophecies were written in the Old Testament from five hundred to one thousand years before the birth of Jesus.)

The place of His birth (Micah 5:2/Matthew 2:1)
The miracle of His birth (Isaiah 7:14/Matthew 1:18)
His triumphal entry (Zechariah 9:9/John 12:13-14)
Betrayed by a friend (Psalm 41:9/Mark 14:10)
His rejection (Isaiah 53:3/John 1:11)
His death with sinners (Isaiah 53:12/Matthew 27:38)
His hands and feet pierced (Psalm 22:16/John 20:27)
He was mocked and ridiculed (Psalm 22:7-8/Luke 23:35)
Soldiers gamble for His clothes (Psalm 22:18/Luke 23:34)
No bones would be broken (Psalm 34:20/John 19:33)
Soldier pierced His side (Zechariah 12:10/ John 19:34)
He would be a sacrifice for sin (Isaiah 53:5-12/Romans 5:6-8)
His resurrection (Psalm 16:10/Acts 3:15)
His ascension (Psalm 68:18/Mark 16:19)

We started this session with the statement: At the end of the day, everyone must answer the question "Who is Jesus?" Everything in this life and the next depends on how you answer that question.

Take some time to consider your personal conclusions about Jesus.

What stands out to you most about Jesus?

What makes Him unique?

What questions are you still wrestling with?

Who do you say He is?

JESUS: FULLY HUMAN

The term "Son of Man" identified Jesus as fully human. You may ask, "Why is this important? Wasn't it obvious that Jesus was human?" During the late second century, a group of people taught that Jesus wasn't fully human; He only "appeared" to be human. One of the early church leaders named Ignatius fought against that erroneous teaching. He wrote that Jesus "was really born, and ate, and drank, was really persecuted by Pontius Pilate, was really crucified and died … and really rose from the dead" (Ignatius, *Epistle to the Trallians* 9).

> *Look up the verses below and identify how Jesus' humanity is seen in each situation.*
>
> *John 4:6-7*
>
> *Luke 2:52*
>
> *John 11:33-35*
>
> *Matthew 4:1-2*
>
> *John 19:28-30*

You may also ask, "What relevance is it for me today that Jesus was fully human?" The answer is simple: Because Jesus experienced every range of human experience—pain and loss, anger and suffering, love and joy, hunger and thirst, temptation and disappointment—He can identify and sympathize with our hurts and weaknesses. Every emotion or experience you have gone through, Jesus has been through. And in your darkest moments you can turn to Him. He understands. He's been there.

Another reason Jesus used the term "Son of Man" for Himself was because this term was a prophetic title given to the Messiah. The Promised One would come from God, deliver people from their sins, and make them right with God. Look at the following prophecy about the coming of the Son of Man.

¹³ I continued watching in the night visions, and I saw One like a son of man coming with the clouds of heaven. He approached the Ancient of Days and was escorted before Him. ¹⁴ He was given authority to rule, and glory, and a kingdom; so that those of every people, nation, and language should serve Him. His dominion is an everlasting dominion that will not pass away, and His kingdom is one that will not be destroyed.
DANIEL 7:13-14

In this vision, how did Daniel describe the Son of Man?

Daniel saw the day coming when the Son of Man would be revealed as the Christ—the Messiah—the One who would bring the people back to God. And this was exactly who Jesus claimed to be. In John 1:41, Andrew found his brother and said, "'We have found the Messiah!' (which means 'Anointed One')." Nathanael declared Jesus as the "King of Israel" (John 1:49), another reference to Jesus as the Messiah.

Read the verses below. How did Jesus claim to be the Messiah?

John 4:25-26

Matthew 16:13-18

Matthew 26:63-64

What stands out to you most about Jesus' title as the "Son of Man"?

What is your reaction to Jesus' claim to be the Christ?

JESUS: FULLY GOD

The Bible gives us several facts about Jesus that prove His divine nature.

First, Scripture tells us that Jesus existed before time. Jesus has always existed. Before time and space, before anything was created, Jesus existed. He existed eternally with God the Father, and through Jesus all things were created. In a confrontation with religious leaders, Jesus said, "You are from below. … I am from above. You are of this world; I am not of this world" (John 8:23). When they appealed to Abraham as their father, Jesus boldly declared, "Before Abraham was, I am" (John 8:58). In that statement He declared Himself to be God, existing before Abraham.

How does Colossians 1:15-20 describe Jesus' preexistence and authority?

Not only did Jesus exist before time and create all things, He chose to come into the world.

¹ In the beginning was the Word, and the Word was with God, and the Word was God. ² He was with God in the beginning. ³ All things were created through Him, and apart from Him not one thing was created that has been created. ⁴ Life was in Him, and that life was the light of men. ⁵ That light shines in the darkness, yet the darkness did not overcome it.

⁹ The true light, who gives light to everyone, was coming into the world. ¹⁰ He was in the world, and the world was created through Him, yet the world did not recognize Him. ¹¹ He came to His own, and His own people did not receive Him. ¹² But to all who did receive Him, He gave them the right to be children of God, to those who believe in His name, ¹³ who were born, not of blood, or of the will of the flesh, or of the will of man, but of God. ¹⁴ The Word became flesh and took up residence among us. We observed His glory, the glory as the One and Only Son from the Father, full of grace and truth.
JOHN 1:1-5,9-14

What promise do we have in verse 12?

Jesus also became a Man. Jesus came into this world, but He didn't come as a conquering king or a wealthy aristocrat. He came as a simple baby, born in a manger. He came in silence, on a clear night, in a small town in Israel called Bethlehem. He was born to common parents. Yet His birth was miraculous. God was becoming one of us.

Look at the birth accounts in Luke and Matthew. How did the angel describe this birth to Mary in Luke 1:26-37?

Why is Jesus given the title "Immanuel" in Matthew 1:20-23?

God came to us in the person of Jesus. He was in every way "God with us." Jesus never ceased to be God, but He emptied Himself (see Phil. 2:7) and became a man so that He could die for our sin on the cross.

Jesus claimed to be God. While the Bible is full of statements about Jesus' identity as God, none are more powerful than the words of Jesus Himself. Take a moment to read Matthew 25:31-32; John 10:22-33; 14:6-7.

How would you summarize the claims Jesus made about Himself in these passages?

Jesus demonstrated His divine power. Jesus not only claimed to have authority, but He also demonstrated His authority in many ways:

- Jesus demonstrated His authority over sickness (see Luke 4:40).
- Jesus demonstrated His authority over demons (see Luke 4:33-36).
- Jesus demonstrated His authority over sin (see Luke 5:20-25).
- Jesus demonstrated His authority over death (see John 11:43-44).

Ultimately, Jesus' greatest demonstration of His authority and the greatest vindication of His claim to be God was His own resurrection from the dead. Jesus told His disciples He would die and be raised to life again (see Matt. 16:21), Jesus was raised from the dead (see Matt. 28:1-10), Jesus showed Himself to His disciples after His resurrection (see Acts 1:1-3; 1 Cor. 15:3-8), and His disciples boldly proclaimed Jesus' resurrection (see Acts 2:29-32; 4:1-2).

WHAT DID JESUS DO?

Jesus is worth following because only
He can solve our deepest problem.

REFLECT

In the previous session we learned about the uniqueness of Jesus. We saw that He is worth following because there is no one like Him. We also saw that He was fully human, yet fully God. And before a person can come to know Christ personally, he or she must answer the question, "Who is Jesus?" As you spent some time over the past week reading, journaling, and reflecting on Jesus, hopefully you had a chance to share some of what you've learned with someone else.

Use the following questions to begin the session with discussion.

Which of the assignments did you explore this week? How did it go?

What did you learn or experience while reading the Bible?

What questions would you like to ask?

PRAY

Begin this session by connecting with God through prayer. Use the following guidelines as you speak with Him together:

- Ask for your eyes to be opened to see what Jesus has done for you in a fresh and new way.

- Pray that God would move your heart to love Jesus more deeply and personally.

- Ask for wisdom as you explore what Jesus has done to heal and restore you.

INTRODUCTION

In the late 1800s scientists and doctors believed that diseases were created by spontaneous generation. The idea was that diseases were random acts that popped up spontaneously from skin or the dust and could kill hundreds or even thousands of people.

Because these diseases were random, they couldn't be predicted or prevented. But a French scientist named Louis Pasteur boldly declared that the medical community had it all wrong. He claimed that there was an invisible world that couldn't be seen by the naked eye. This world was a world of microorganisms. These micro-organisms could float through the air, attach themselves to food, be passed from person to person, or sit on contaminated objects and carry disease.

Immediately those who believed the research started washing their hands, separating the sick from the healthy, and covering their mouths when they coughed. But others scoffed at Pasteur's idea. The thought that there was an unseen world that was causing the problems of illness and death seemed strange. Today we know that Pasteur was right, and his groundbreaking research in germ theory paved the way for vaccines that have saved millions of lives.

In a similar way, the Bible tells us that we have an unseen problem. We see the effects of this problem every day. We live in a world full of crime, abuse, disease, promiscuity, rage, violence, and deceit. But while these things are bad in and of themselves, they're only symptoms of a deeper problem—a soul sickness. This soul sickness causes brokenness in our relationships on earth and brokenness in our relationship with the God of heaven. In this session we're going to discover that Jesus came to earth to solve our problem. He came to heal our soul sickness, to be the antidote that will restore people back to one another and back to God.

Where do you see evidence of soul sickness in today's culture? In your community?

What are some ways people try to solve this soul problem?

KNOW THE STORY

Nicodemus, a deeply religious man and member of Israel's highest ruling council, came to Jesus with questions on his mind. In this brief conversation, Jesus revealed the truth about who He is and why He came to earth.

2 "Rabbi, we know that You have come from God as a teacher, for no one could perform these signs You do unless God were with him." 3 Jesus replied, "I assure you: Unless someone is born again, he cannot see the kingdom of God." 4 "But how can anyone be born when he is old?" Nicodemus asked Him. "Can he enter his mother's womb a second time and be born?" 5 Jesus answered, "I assure you: Unless someone is born of water and the Spirit, he cannot enter the kingdom of God. 6 Whatever is born of the flesh is flesh, and whatever is born of the Spirit is spirit. 7 Do not be amazed that I told you that you must be born again. 8 The wind blows where it pleases, and you hear its sound, but you don't know where it comes from or where it is going. So it is with everyone born of the Spirit." 9 "How can these things be?" asked Nicodemus. 10 "Are you a teacher of Israel and don't know these things?" Jesus replied. 11 "I assure you: We speak what We know and We testify to what We have seen, but you do not accept Our testimony. 12 If I have told you about things that happen on earth and you don't believe, how will you believe if I tell you about things of heaven? 13 No one has ascended into heaven except the One who descended from heaven—the Son of Man. 14 Just as Moses lifted up the snake in the wilderness, so the Son of Man must be lifted up, 15 so that everyone who believes in Him will have eternal life. 16 "For God loved the world in this way: He gave His One and Only Son, so that everyone who believes in Him will not perish but have eternal life. 17 For God did not send His Son into the world that He might condemn the world, but that the world might be saved through Him."
JOHN 3:2-17

What are some of the larger themes expressed in these verses?

What can we learn about Jesus from these verses?

UNPACK THE STORY

OUR PROBLEM

Jesus came to solve a problem, a spiritual problem. More specifically, *our* spiritual problem. But like many people today, Nicodemus was unaware that he had a problem. In his own estimation, he was a good, morally religious man. What could be his problem? But Jesus knew something that Nicodemus did not know. Jesus knew Nicodemus had a problem that was keeping him from knowing God deeply and personally.

Read the following passages. What is the problem? Who has this problem? What does this problem mean for us?

Romans 3:10-18,23

Ephesians 2:1

Romans 6:23

Like many people today, Nicodemus was unaware that he had a problem. In his own estimation, he was a good, morally religious man.

Nicodemus came to Jesus at night—in secret. He had questions for Jesus. He heard stories and wanted to know if Jesus was the real thing. And sometimes we may wonder the same thing. Does faith make sense? We may doubt. We're often uncertain.

When Jesus spoke to Nicodemus, He cut straight to the heart of the problem. With all his morality and religion, Nicodemus was a sinful man who desperately needed to start over. He was a man who needed to be changed from the inside out.

Describe the time when you first became aware of your own sinfulness.

GOD'S SOLUTION

When Jesus spoke with Nicodemus, He predicted His death on the cross when He said "the Son of Man must be lifted up" (John 3:14). This was God's solution to our problem. Jesus died as the full and final payment for our sin. Because the penalty of sin is death (see Rom. 6:23; Heb. 9:22), God chose to put our sin on Jesus to die as our substitute. On the cross, God poured out His wrath toward sin on Jesus, and He suffered in our place.

In what ways does the fact that Jesus took on your sin and died as your substitute affect your life?

Jesus told Nicodemus the reason for His death. Read His words again:

> For God loved the world in this way: He gave His One and Only Son, so that everyone who believes in Him will not perish but have eternal life.
> **JOHN 3:16**

Romans 5:8 says, "God proves His own love for us in that while we were still sinners, Christ died for us!" Thinking about God's great love, the apostle Paul wrote these words:

> [38] For I am persuaded that not even death or life, angels or rulers, things present or things to come, hostile powers, [39] height or depth, or any other created thing will have the power to separate us from the love of God that is in Christ Jesus our Lord!
> **ROMANS 8:38-39**

Romans 5:8 says, "God proves His own love for us in that while we were still sinners, Christ died for us!"

Think about it. God sent Jesus, His only Son, to die in our place so that by His sacrifice we could be forgiven, restored, and made new again. And He did it all because He loves you. It was God's love that sent Jesus to earth. It was God's love that compelled Jesus to the cross. And it is God's love that draws us back to Him.

ENGAGE

During His conversation with Jesus, Nicodemus learned that it's not enough to be a good, moral, or even religious person. Everyone has a sin problem. And only Jesus can solve that problem. Jesus told Nicodemus, "You must be born again." When He said that He certainly didn't mean that a person must be born again in the literal sense. Jesus was speaking about a new birth. Just as a person is born physically, a person must also be born spiritually. When we turn from sin and turn to Jesus, we are born again. We can start over. We can become a new person (see 2 Cor. 5:17).

Spend time discussing what you've learned from the story of Jesus and Nicodemus and how it relates to your own story. Use the following questions as a guide for sharing your testimony.

What was your life like before you came to know Jesus?

Have you "passed from death to life" (John 5:24)? Be as specific as you can, sharing how you came to faith in Jesus.

Share briefly the difference Jesus has made in your life.

PRAYER REQUESTS

In addition to studying God's Word, work with your group leader to create a plan for personal study, worship, and application between now and the next session. Select from the following optional activities to match your personal preferences and available time.

⬆ Worship

☑ Read your Bible. Complete the reading plan on page 30.

☐ Connect with God by engaging the devotional on page 31.

☐ Take time to read through the story of Jesus' death and resurrection found in Matthew 26:14–28:20. As you read it, pause to worship Jesus along the way.

➡ ⬅ Personal Study

☐ Read and interact with "Our Problem" on page 32

☐ Read and interact with "God's Solution" on page 34.

⬅ ➡ Application

☐ Connect with others. Tell someone one thing you learned from this session. You may want to take the memory verse you are learning this week and share it with your neighbors, spouse, or children.

☐ Memorize 1 Corinthians 15:3-5: "For I passed on to you as most important what I also received: that Christ died for our sins according to the Scriptures, that He was buried, that He was raised on the third day according to the Scriptures, and that He appeared to Cephas, then to the Twelve."

☐ Spend time journaling. Write down your personal salvation story. Craft a letter or email that tells what your life was like before you came to Christ, how you heard the gospel, when you prayed to receive Christ by faith, and the difference Jesus has made in your life. Then pray about ways you can share your story with a friend or family member.

☐ Other:

WORSHIP

READING PLAN

Read through the following Scripture passages this week. Use the space provided to record your thoughts and responses.

Day 1
Psalm 34:1-22

Day 2
Isaiah 53:1-12

Day 3
John 10:1-21

Day 4
John 17:1-26

Day 5
2 Corinthians 5:1-21

Day 6
Ephesians 1:1-23

Day 7
Colossians 2:1-23

IN CHRIST ALONE

In 2002, songwriters Stuart Townend and Keith Getty sat down to collaborate on a new worship song. Getty proposed the tune that had a powerful and haunting sound, and Townend composed the lyrics that encompassed the themes of Jesus' life, death, and resurrection.

In an interview Townend said, "We've had some incredible emails about how people have been helped by the song through incredibly difficult circumstances."[1] One email came from an American soldier in Iraq who would pray the lyrics of this song every day and saw God's miraculous protection on the battlefield. The power of this song comes from the fact that its lyrics are rooted in the truth of God's Word.

Here are just a few of the lyrics from "In Christ Alone" that likely comforted the soldier in Iraq:

> What heights of love, what depths of peace,
> when fears are stilled, when strivings cease!
> My Comforter, my All in All,
> here in the love of Christ I stand.[2]

If you haven't heard this song or want to be reminded of it's biblically-rooted lyrics, take a moment to search for the lyrics in their entirety on *hymnary.org*. Listen to the song or read over the words and ponder the hymn's rich meaning. This is a great way to worship Jesus and thank Him for all He has done for us.

Have you ever had a biblically-rooted song, book, or poem that has given you comfort during a difficult circumstance? If so, what was it, and what made it comforting?

Take the time now to find a verse from Scripture or a line from a biblically-rooted song and write it down below. Spend time meditating on those words, and speak them aloud in a prayer to God.

1. Debra Akins, "Song Story: 'In Christ Alone,'" Crosswalk.com. July 22, 2005. Available at: www.crosswalk.com.
2. Keith Getty and Stuart Townend, "In Christ Alone," *Baptist Hymnal* (Nashville, TN: LifeWay Worship, 2008), 506.

OUR PROBLEM

The term *sin* was an archery term in ancient times. It simply means "to miss the mark." God created us to know Him, love Him, and honor Him in everything we do. But when we sin, we miss the mark of knowing, loving, and honoring God. Simply put, sin is anything that displeases God. When we break God's commands, ignore His teaching, rebel against His leadership, or put other things above Him in our lives, we sin against Him.

What questions do you have about sin?

At the core, sin is a heart issue. Someone once said that when you spell the word *sin*, the letter *I* is in the middle. And when I sin against God it's all about what I want, what I need, and what I desire. Pleasing myself takes the place of pleasing God. This sin problem beats in the heart of every person.

- Sin corrupts everything it touches.
- Sin destroys everything that's good.
- Sin perverts everything that's beautiful.
- Sin is at the core of every social and moral problem we face today.
- Sin is the reason we have prisons and rehab.
- Sin is behind every case of evil and injustice.
- Sin is the root cause of every addiction, enslavement, and abuse.
- Sin is why we suffer.
- Sin is why we feel alone.
- Sin is why we face sorrow, sickness, and death.
- Sin enslaves us and keeps us from God.

How do you see the effects of sin in our world today?

How have you experienced the effects of sin in your own life?

Much of the Bible addresses this sin problem and what it means for us. Read the following verses and journal your observations in the space provided.

> I know, LORD, that a man's way of life is not his own; no one who walks determines his own steps.
> **JEREMIAH 10:23**

> Then after desire has conceived, it gives birth to sin, and when sin is fully grown, it gives birth to death.
> **JAMES 1:15**

> So it is a sin for the person who knows to do what is good and doesn't do it.
> **JAMES 4:17**

> If we say, "We have no sin," we are deceiving ourselves, and the truth is not in us.
> **1 JOHN 1:8**

GOD'S SOLUTION

The bad news of the Bible is that we have a sin problem. But the good news of the Bible is that God stepped in to solve our problem and to draw us back to Him. He did this by sending Jesus to us.

The New Testament tells us of Christ's coming in great detail—including why He came:

- **Matthew 1:21:** The angel Gabriel tells Mary about Jesus' mission in life.
- **Luke 19:10:** Jesus tells us His purpose in coming into the world.
- **Romans 5:8:** God demonstrates His love for us in Christ.
- **2 Corinthians 5:21:** Jesus came to be sin for us.
- **John 10:17-18:** Jesus went to the cross willingly.

We don't just see Jesus in the New Testament. Seven hundred years before the death of Jesus, the prophet Isaiah spoke about Jesus' death on the cross. Read Isaiah 53:4-6. As you read these verses, think about what Jesus endured on the cross for you.

> ⁴ Yet He Himself bore our sicknesses,
> and He carried our pains;
> but we in turn regarded Him stricken,
> struck down by God, and afflicted.
> ⁵ But He was pierced because of our transgressions,
> crushed because of our iniquities;
> punishment for our peace was on Him,
> and we are healed by His wounds.
> ⁶ We all went astray like sheep;
> we all have turned to our own way;
> and the LORD has punished Him
> for the iniquity of us all.
> ISAIAH 53:4-6

How does God's love demonstrated at the cross bring you reassurance and hope?

But Jesus' death on the cross isn't the full story. Jesus physically rose from the dead. And that is why Jesus is worth following, because no one else has done what He did. No one else paid our penalty for sin, dying on the cross and rising again from the dead.

Read the following passages and note how each points to God's solution to our sin through Christ's death on the cross.

John 5:24

Romans 10:9-10

Ephesians 2:8-10

2 Corinthians 5:17

Jesus stands head and shoulders above any other religious leader in history. All other religions in some capacity are based on the works and efforts of the individual. Salvation, forgiveness, and reconciliation are dependent on your performance—what you *do*. This includes the prayers you pray, the money you give, and the religious rituals you perform.

But Christianity is based on what has already been *done*. It's all about what Jesus has done for us!

In John 9:4, Jesus says, "We must do the works of Him who sent Me while it is day. Night is coming when no one can work." Then in John 19:30 Jesus declared on the cross, "It is finished." His work of reconciliation, satisfying the Father's justice against sin and opening up a way for people to be right with God, was finished. Any good works we do aren't to earn God's approval or to obtain forgiveness, but rather to express love and gratitude for all Jesus has done for us.

FOLLOWING JESUS

Jesus calls every person to follow Him.

REFLECT

In the last session, we looked at the work of Jesus and we discovered that He is worth following because He is the One who came to solve our deepest problem. Only Jesus died for our sin, rose from the dead, and offers life here and in the hereafter. Hopefully you had the opportunity to do additional study this week, reflect on the work of Jesus, and even share what you learned. Take a moment to talk about what you learned this week.

Use the following questions to begin the session with discussion.

Which of the assignments did you explore this week? How did it go?

What did you learn or experience while reading the Bible?

What questions would you like to ask?

PRAY

Before you dive into this session, stop and pray together as a group. Use the following guidelines as you speak with the Lord together:

- Praise Jesus for all He has done for you.

- Ask Him to forgive you for any area of sin you have allowed to control your life this past week.

- Seek Him for His provision in your life and for those in your group. Cast your cares on Him because He cares for you (see 1 Pet. 5:7).

- Give the rest of your time together to Jesus, asking Him to teach you and grow you.

INTRODUCTION

In 2006, the small upstart podcast company Odeo was struggling to stay alive. Just as it was about to launch a new product, Apple, Inc. came out with iTunes®, which included a robust podcast component. Odeo was dead before it even had a chance to truly live.

With only a handful of employees, the company's founder Noah Glass started day-long brainstorming sessions, trying to reinvent itself. In one session, Jack Dorsey, a web designer and one of the first employees of Odeo, had a new idea. Along with Glass, the two dreamed of a product that would allow a person to send a 140-character text message to multiple people at one time. Twitter® was born.

So how does it work? Twitter is an online presence for individuals and companies to easily send information—called "tweets"—to their "followers." This information can be anything from a humorous quote to a link to an interesting blog to an advertisement for the latest product or service, as long as it's within the 140-character limit. A user is then able to control what information they see based on who they choose to follow. They are also able to encourage other users to follow them.[1]

Jesus' favorite invitation was simply, "Follow Me." He invited people from all backgrounds, walks of life, and ages to be His followers. In just a few years, His followers were multiplying around the globe.

But following Jesus is different than being a "follower" on Twitter. Following Jesus changes everything—your life and your world. Today, we're going to learn what it really means to be a follower of Jesus Christ.

What comes to your mind when you hear someone say they are a follower of Jesus?

What do you think is required of a fully-devoted disciple of Jesus?

KNOW THE STORY

The global company known today as Twitter started with a few people who followed the vision and dream of its company founder. Within a few years, Twitter was a global player shaping our culture and the next generation.

In much the same way, the Christian movement had small beginnings. Jesus called a few people to drop what they were doing and sell out to His vision—and the rest is history.

¹⁸ As He was walking along the Sea of Galilee, He saw two brothers, Simon, who was called Peter, and his brother Andrew. They were casting a net into the sea, since they were fishermen. ¹⁹ "Follow Me," He told them, "and I will make you fish for people!" ²⁰ Immediately they left their nets and followed Him. ²¹ Going on from there, He saw two other brothers, James the son of Zebedee, and his brother John. They were in a boat with Zebedee their father, mending their nets, and He called them. ²² Immediately they left the boat and their father and followed Him.
MATTHEW 4:18-22

What is your reaction to the response of the fishermen?

What does their response tell you about them?

Are you still preparing your net or are you ready to leave the boat? Explain.

UNPACK THE STORY

A LINE IN THE SAND

Just reading this passage at face value, a person could easily think this was the first meeting Jesus had with these men. But it wasn't. The fact is Peter, Andrew, James, and John had been casual followers of Jesus for the past year and a half.

The Gospel of John fills in this gap between Matthew 4:17 and 4:18. We've already seen that Jesus first met Andrew, John, and Peter immediately following His temptation (see John 1:35-42). At that point these men, along with Philip and Nathanael, began to follow Jesus. Think of them as Jesus' starting five! They went with Him to Cana where Jesus performed His first miracle, turning water to wine (see John 2:1-11). Afterward Jesus traveled with these men to Jerusalem to celebrate the Passover. There Jesus turned over the money changer tables (see John 2:13-17), encountered a Pharisee named Nicodemus (see John 3:1-16), and met a Samaritan woman by a well (see John 4:1-26).

But now after well over a year, Jesus was ready to call these men to a higher level of commitment.

Matthew 4:20, 22 state that "immediately they left" what they were doing and followed Jesus. Why do you think they felt such urgency?

> Jesus was calling them to leave behind their old way of life and follow Him fully and completely. He was drawing a line in the sand and asking them to follow Him without reservation.

Up to this point, these men had been investigating the claims of Jesus. They had been learning His identity—He was fully God and fully man. Although they didn't comprehend it all, they were also growing in their understanding of the work Jesus came to do. But now Jesus was calling them to leave behind their old way of life and follow Him fully and completely. He was drawing a line in the sand and asking them to follow Him without reservation.

How have you responded to Jesus' call for commitment?

A DISCIPLE WHO MAKES DISCIPLES

From this point forward, Jesus began to prioritize His time with these new disciples. Just reading through the Bible, we find Jesus with the crowd 17 times but 46 times alone with His disciples.

It's clear that Jesus' strategy was not to *reach* the world, but to *train* disciples who would reach the world. Jesus' goal was not to *change* the world, but to *raise up* disciples who would change the world forever.

In what ways are you making yourself available to be raised up and trained?

A few chapters later, Jesus commissioned His disciples again saying:

> [37] The harvest is abundant, but the workers are few.
> [38] Therefore, pray to the Lord of the harvest to send out workers into His harvest.
> MATTHEW 9:37-38

As you work through this study, not only are you growing and learning how to become a disciple of Jesus, but you are also being trained to make disciples.

What's your biggest obstacle to becoming a disciple who makes other disciples?

Jesus' goal was not to *change* the world, but to *raise up* disciples who would change the world forever.

ENGAGE

The apostle Paul was a disciple of Jesus Christ. When he met Jesus on the road to Damascus, his life was radically changed. From that moment on, he was determined to know Jesus deeply and personally and to join Jesus in His mission to make disciples who make disciples.

Read aloud the following excerpt from Paul's letter to the church at Philippi. As a group, reflect on his words. Discuss how you can apply them to your own desire to know and follow Jesus.

[7] Everything that was a gain to me, I have considered to be a loss because of Christ. [8] More than that, I also consider everything to be a loss in view of the surpassing value of knowing Christ Jesus my Lord. Because of Him I have suffered the loss of all things and consider them filth, so that I may gain Christ [9] and be found in Him, not having a righteousness of my own from the law, but one that is through faith in Christ—the righteousness from God based on faith. [10] My goal is to know Him and the power of His resurrection and the fellowship of His sufferings, being conformed to His death, [11] assuming that I will somehow reach the resurrection from among the dead. [12] Not that I have already reached the goal or am already fully mature, but I make every effort to take hold of it because I also have been taken hold of by Christ Jesus. [13] Brothers, I do not consider myself to have taken hold of it. But one thing I do: Forgetting what is behind and reaching forward to what is ahead, [14] I pursue as my goal the prize promised by God's heavenly call in Christ Jesus.
PHILIPPIANS 3:7-14

PRAYER REQUESTS

....

....

....

....

....

....

....

1. Nicholas Carlson, "The Real History of Twitter," www.businessinsider.com, April 13, 2011.

In addition to studying God's Word, work with your group leader to create a plan for personal study, worship, and application between now and the next session. Select from the following optional activities to match your personal preferences and available time.

⬆ Worship

☑ Read your Bible. Complete the reading plan on page 44.

☐ Connect with God by engaging the devotional on page 45.

☐ Talk with God each day this week. Every morning, commit several minutes to prayer. Ask God to help you understand what it looks like to be His disciple. Use the following prayer as a starting point: "Dear Jesus, allow me to recognize Your calling on my life and to respond with urgency. Release barriers in my life that prevent me from running after You. Continually grow me into a disciple that makes other disciples."

➡ ⬅ Personal Study

☐ Read and interact with "3 D's of a True Disciple" on page 46.

☐ Read and interact with "Fishing Lessons" on page 48.

⬅ ➡ Application

☐ Engage with others. Make a short list of people in your life with whom you think God wants you to engage. Pray that God will give you opportunities to invest in their lives by carrying out the principle of disciples making disciples.

☐ Memorize Matthew 4:19: " 'Follow Me' [Jesus] told them, 'and I will make you fish for people.' "

☐ Spend time journaling. Write down your reflections on the following statements:
The moment I met Jesus my life was _____.
To follow Jesus and be His disciple will require me to _____.
I want to join Him in His mission, but I am often held back by _____.

☐ Other:

 **WORSHIP**

READING PLAN

Read through the following Scripture passages this week. Use the space provided to record your thoughts and responses.

Day 1
Mark 10:17-31

Day 2
Mark 16:14-20

Day 3
Luke 9:57-62

Day 4
Luke 10:25-37

Day 5
John 15:1-17

Day 6
Romans 10:1-18

Day 7
2 Timothy 2:1-26

A DECLARATION OF FAITH

The following letter was written by an African pastor from Zimbabwe. It was found in his desk after he was martyred for his faith in Jesus. Take time to read it and reflect on the meaning in this powerful declaration.

I'm part of the fellowship of the unashamed, I have the Holy Spirit power, the die has been cast, I have stepped over the line, the decision has been made: I'm a disciple of Jesus Christ. I won't look back, let up, slow down, back away, or be still.

My past is redeemed, my present makes sense, my future is secure. I'm finished and done with low living, sight walking, smooth knees, colorless dreams, tamed visions, worldly talking, cheap giving, and dwarfed goals.

I no longer need preeminence, prosperity, position, promotions, plaudits, or popularity. I do not have to be right, first, tops, recognized, praised, regarded, or rewarded. I now live by faith, lean in His presence, walk by patience, am uplifted by prayer, and I labor with power.

My face is set, my gait is fast, my goal is heaven, my road is narrow, my way rough, my companions are few, my guide is reliable, my mission is clear. I won't give up, shut up, let up until I have stayed up, stored up, prayed up for the cause of Jesus Christ.

I must go till He comes, give till I drop, preach till everyone knows, work till He stops me, and when He comes for His own, He will have no trouble recognizing me because my banner will have been clear.[1]

Journal your observations from this letter below.

3 D'S OF A TRUE DISCIPLE

A 3-D object is fully formed. It's not a flat, one-dimensional image or even two-dimensional with only length and width. It's fully formed with length, width, and depth, and usually lifelike. Jesus never called for some kind of one-dimensional, shallow commitment or lip service. He was looking for fully devoted followers. So let's use three Ds to define a true disciple of Jesus. A true disciple is:

1. Devoted to Jesus. Jesus said, "Follow Me … and I will make you fish for people" (Matt. 4:19). Jesus' favorite invitation was simply, "Follow Me." He used it 24 times in the Gospels. Jesus called Peter, Andrew, James, and John to follow Him, and they dropped everything. He spoke those words to Matthew, the hated tax collector, and Matthew left everything to follow Jesus (see Mark 2:14). The same invitation was extended to Philip from Bethsaida, and he followed Jesus (see John 1:43). He spoke those words to casual observers who praised Him with their words but were unwilling to change their lifestyles (see Luke 9:59-62). He even spoke that invitation to a wealthy, young ruler who chose to hold onto his own money and power rather than follow Jesus (see Mark 10:21-22). Jesus invited everyone to follow Him. But what does it mean to "follow Jesus"? For starters, it means to be devoted to Jesus by placing your trust and faith in Him for salvation.

> *How do Matthew 4:17; Acts 2:36-41; and Ephesians 2:8-9 describe how a person becomes a follower of Jesus?*

2. Developing the attitudes and priorities of Jesus. Jesus saw the potential in these fishermen, but it would take time with Jesus to develop them into trained followers. Over the next two years, they would begin to develop the same attitudes and priories as Jesus.

Love for one another:
By this all people will know that you are My disciples, if you have love for one another.
JOHN 13:35

Self denial, even death:
34 Summoning the crowd along with His disciples, He said to them, "If anyone wants to be My follower, he must deny himself, take up his cross, and follow Me. 35 For whoever wants to save his life will lose it, but whoever loses his life because of Me and the gospel will save it."
MARK 8:34-35

Learning and living the Word of God:

³¹ If you continue in My word, you really are My disciples. ³² You will know the truth, and the truth will set you free.
JOHN 8:31-32

Allegiance to Jesus above all other allegiances:

²⁵ Now great crowds were traveling with Him. So He turned and said to them: ²⁶ "If anyone comes to Me and does not hate his own father and mother, wife and children, brothers and sisters—yes, and even his own life—he cannot be My disciple. ²⁷ Whoever does not bear his own cross and come after Me cannot be My disciple."
LUKE 14:25-27

Would you say that the character and priorities of Jesus are being reflected in your life? Why or why not?

3. Deployed to make disciples who make disciples. Jesus said, "Follow Me … and I will make you fish for people!" (Matt. 4:19). No longer were these men going to settle for just fishing; now they were going to fish for people. From this point forward they were going to be captivated by a greater vision of multiplying disciples and taking the message of Jesus across the globe. And this is the same vision Jesus cast to His disciples throughout all generations.

¹⁸ Jesus came near and said to them, "All authority has been given to Me in heaven and on earth. ¹⁹ Go, therefore, and make disciples of all nations, baptizing them in the name of the Father and of the Son and of the Holy Spirit, ²⁰ teaching them to observe everything I have commanded you. And remember, I am with you always, to the end of the age."
MATTHEW 28:18-20

A disciple is a person who is devoted to Jesus, developing the character/priorities of Jesus, and deployed to make disciples who make disciples. A true disciple is devoted, developed, and deployed.

In what areas of life have you experienced consistent spiritual growth? In what areas do you still need to grow?

FISHING LESSONS

The word *disciple* is a term used for a follower of Jesus. It's an important word. It comes from the Greek word *mathetes,* which means "a learner." In Jesus' day a disciple was a person who followed a master to learn from him and to ultimately carry out his work. The Hebrew word *taladim* carried the same meaning: "a learner." It was often used to describe a scholar or rabbi in training. So *disciple* became the first word used to describe the followers of Jesus. It appears at least 230 times in the Gospels and 28 times in the Book of Acts. But what does a true disciple of Jesus look like?

In Luke 4:31–5:31 Jesus led His disciples on six "fishing trips" to train them how to fish for people. Read and study each passage and write down what lessons the disciples are learning about "fishing." Notice who they are fishing for, what they do, and the final result.

Fishing trip 1—Luke 4:31-37

Fishing trip 2—Luke 4:38-44

Fishing trip 3—Luke 5:1-11

Fishing Trip 4—Luke 5:12-16

Fishing Trip 5—Luke 5:17-26

Fishing Trip 6—Luke 5:27-31

What has God been teaching you about your own "fishing"? What is He instructing you to do? God has likely been taking you on your own fishing trip and has been equipping you with gospel nets to cast out. He is training you and teaching you concerning what it means to follow after Him. How will you respond?

1. As quoted in Rod Dempsy, *Disciple Making Is ... How to Live the Great Commission with Passion and Confidence* (Nashville, TN: B&H Publishing Group, 2013), 90.

THE PRIORITIES OF A DISCIPLE

Following Jesus means living a life that reflects His character and priorities.

GET STARTED

REFLECT

In the last session, we examined how Jesus invites people from all backgrounds, walks of life, and ages to be His followers. We also looked at how following Jesus changes everything—our lives and our world. We learned what it *really* means to be a follower of Jesus Christ. Hopefully you had the opportunity to do additional study this week and reflect on what it means to be a follower of Jesus.

Use the following questions to begin the session with discussion.

Which of the assignments did you explore this week? How did it go?

What did you learn or experience while reading the Bible?

What questions would you like to ask?

PRAY

Today we are going to talk about the priorities of a disciple of Jesus Christ. Before you dive into this session, stop and pray together as a group. Use the following guidelines as you speak with the Lord together:

- Seek after Him with an open heart and mind to receive what He has for you today.

- Ask God to reveal the priorities He wants you to have in your life.

- Pray for one another and for God's leadership in your lives.

INTRODUCTION

Shawn Klush is probably not a name you recognize. He was raised in a small coal-mining town in Pittston, Pennsylvania. Klush holds the title as the best Elvis impersonator in the world. In 2005, Klush became the grand champion at the World Elvis Tribute Artist Competition and was named the international champion of the BBC's World's Greatest Elvis Competition by more than 6.5 million viewers in the United Kingdom.

Currently Klush tours extensively, has produced three albums, and appears frequently in Las Vegas. Klush shared in an interview that he began imitating Elvis at the age of 2, but honed his imitating skills over time.[1] He says, "It's a natural thing for me to do. I say that with the utmost respect. It just comes very easy for me. I ran with it, not realizing it. Finally, after a long time, I realized, 'Wow, this is what I was supposed to do.'"[2]

Imitation is the greatest form of flattery, and true disciples of Jesus Christ are people who are committed to imitating Jesus. Over and over, Jesus told His followers to do what He did, live as He lived, and walk as He walked (see John 6:57; John 13:34; John 14:12; John 15:10; John 17:18; and John 20:21). Jesus said in Luke 6:40, "A disciple is not above his teacher, but everyone who is fully trained will be like his teacher." On another occasion Jesus said, "I have given you an example that you also should do just as I have done for you" (John 13:15). First John 2:6 says, "The one who says he remains in Him should walk just as He walked."

All through Scripture we are told that God's plan for us is to be like Jesus. Romans 8:29 says God's plan is that we be "conformed to the image of His Son." The apostle Peter encouraged believers to follow in the steps of Jesus (see 1 Pet. 2:21). The apostle Paul said that he was going to keep working hard "until Christ is formed in you" (Gal. 4:19). And he told believers in Corinth, "Imitate me, as I also imitate Christ" (1 Cor. 11:1). God's plan for every Christ-follower is Christlikeness.

In what ways can a person imitate Jesus today?

What do you think is hardest about trying to live like Jesus?

KNOW THE STORY

Two years passed since Peter and Andrew first met Jesus. For the first year and a half, they followed Jesus at a distance, exploring His claims and coming to the conviction that Jesus was the Christ, the Son of God (see Matt. 16:16). Then they answered His call to "follow Him" and become fishers of people. During the next several months Peter, Andrew, James, and John shadowed Jesus, watching Him do miracles, heal the sick, cast out demons, and confront the religious establishment of the day. They were on a steep learning curve for sure!

But now Jesus was raising the stakes again. Two years into His ministry, the movement was growing so rapidly that Jesus needed to identify and train a few disciples who would lead the movement once He was gone. He spent all night in prayer, asking the Father for wisdom as He selected these disciples. Then He chose 12. Jesus would train these disciples for the next year and a half. Eventually, they would take the gospel to the ends of the earth.

[13] He went up the mountain and summoned those He wanted, and they came to Him. [14] He also appointed 12—He also named them apostles—to be with Him, to send them out to preach, [15] and to have authority to drive out demons. [16] He appointed the Twelve: To Simon, He gave the name Peter; [17] and to James the son of Zebedee, and to his brother John, He gave the name "Boanerges" (that is, "Sons of Thunder"); [18] Andrew; Philip and Bartholomew; Matthew and Thomas; James the son of Alphaeus, and Thaddaeus; Simon the Zealot, [19] and Judas Iscariot, who also betrayed Him.

MARK 3:13-19

Based on these verses, what qualities do you think Jesus was looking for in these disciples?

What does it mean to be "with Him"? To be "sent out" by Him?

UNPACK THE STORY

JESUS USES ORDINARY PEOPLE

Jesus hand-selected these disciples to be leaders. They were an interesting group to say the least. None were wealthy, highly educated, powerful, or from the ranks of the religious elite. In fact, the opposite is true. Most were hard-working laborers, others were political zealots, one was a dishonest tax collector, and still others were small-town nobodies.

Look at the way Acts 4:13 refers to Peter and John:

> When they observed the boldness of Peter and John and realized that they were uneducated and untrained men, they were amazed and recognized that they had been with Jesus.
> **ACTS 4:13**

These uneducated, common men were transformed by Jesus. That should bring us a lot of comfort. Jesus loves using common, ordinary people to do uncommon, extraordinary things!

Jesus loves using common, ordinary people to do uncommon, extraordinary things!

Being a follower of Christ doesn't mean we always do extraordinary things for God. What are some ordinary things a follower of Christ can do to advance the kingdom?

Jesus instilled His priorities and His character into His disciples. The end result was that they were fully trained to carry on the ministry Jesus began. Examine the following training experiences Jesus had with His disciples:

Matthew 11:2-19—How did Jesus train these disciples to deal with doubt?

Luke 7:36-50—How did Jesus train these disciples to exercise forgiveness?

JESUS DRAWS IN AND SENDS OUT

In Mark 3:14 we get a glimpse of Jesus' leadership training plan. Look at it again. Jesus called these disciples to be with Him and to send them out to preach. Jesus' leadership training plan was twofold. First, He chose these disciples so He could "be with them." He wanted to draw them close to Himself, so they could learn in a deeper way about His power and authority over all things.

Describe a time in your past when you were mentored by someone.

Was this time beneficial to you? Explain.

Over the next six to nine months, Jesus taught the Twelve what it means to be a part of God's kingdom work. Jesus preached His two greatest sermons and taught repeatedly through parables and stories. He demonstrated His power over sickness, nature, and even the demonic. Jesus stretched their minds and exposed them to God's heart for the nations. But most of all, Jesus pulled these disciples close enough to see and embrace His priorities.

Second, Jesus sent the disciples out. He was preparing these disciples to go out and do what He was doing. It would be on-the-job training, not just a classroom education. They got their hands dirty in ministry and eventually were released to go out on their own and do what He had trained them to do.

Read Matthew 10:5-23. Discuss your observations about this passage in terms of being sent out.

Jesus was preparing these disciples to go out and do what He was doing. They got their hands dirty in ministry and eventually were released to go out on their own and do what He had trained them to do.

ENGAGE

We have already seen that love is a priority of Jesus. Jesus taught us to love, especially those who can't repay or reward us.

> Pure and undefiled religion before our God and Father is this: to look after orphans and widows in their distress and to keep oneself unstained by the world.
> JAMES 1:27

Take a moment to brainstorm how your group can practically demonstrate God's love to widows, orphans, and needy people in your community. Make some plans to put love into action.

Ways to demonstrate God's love:

To widows:

To orphans:

To those in need:

PRAYER REQUESTS

....

....

....

....

1. Available from the internet: www.shawnklush.com. Accessed May 13, 2015
2. Jeff Niesel, "King for a Day: Shawn Klush Reflects on a Lifetime of Imitating Elvis," *Cleveland Scene,* January 8, 2014. Available online at clevescene.com. Accessed April 30, 2015.

In addition to studying God's Word, work with your group leader to create a plan for personal study, worship, and application between now and the next session. Select from the following optional activities to match your personal preferences and available time.

⬆ Worship

☑ Read your Bible. Complete the reading plan on page 58.

☐ Connect with God by engaging the devotional on page 59.

☐ Jesus had a habit of getting up early in the morning before daylight to pray. Experiment with this by waking up a few mornings this week before sunrise to worship God. You might choose some psalms to read or play worship music. Praise God for what He's done in your life. Ask Him to search your heart and reveal anything that's not pleasing to Him. Give Him your cares and concerns. Close your time by asking the Spirit to fill you and use you that day.

➡ ⬅ Personal Study

☐ Read and interact with "Jesus' Upward Priorities" on page 60.

☐ Read and interact with "Jesus' Outward Priorities" on page 62.

⬅ ➡ Application

☐ Spend some time journaling. Right on the heels of Jesus choosing His leaders, He preached one of His greatest sermons. The sermon is all about how to live like Jesus with a kingdom mindset. Take time this week to read through this sermon in Matthew 5–7. Write down your observations. What stands out to you? What questions were raised? What action do you feel God leading you to take as a result of reading this sermon?

☐ Reach out to a friend this week. Take him or her to lunch and share the priorities of Jesus you have learned. Talk about what priorities need to change in your life in order to begin to walk as Jesus walked.

☐ Memorize 1 John 2:6: "The one who says he remains in Him should walk just as He walked."

☐ Other:

 **WORSHIP**

READING PLAN

Read through the following Scripture passages this week. Use the space provided to record your thoughts and responses.

Day 1
Romans 8:1-30

Day 2
Romans 13:1-14

Day 3
Galatians 4:1-20

Day 4
Ephesians 4:1-16

Day 5
Ephesians 4:17-32

Day 6
1 Peter 2:11-25

Day 7
Colossians 3:1-17

GLASS VASE OF PRIORITIES

According to *Merriam-Webster's Collegiate Dictionary*, the definition of *priority* is "something requiring or meriting attention prior to competing alternatives." A priority is something that is *most* important. It's something that takes first place and is of greater value than anything else. When you look at the life of Jesus you will recognize that God's Word, prayer, obedience, love, and investing in others were the priorities of His life. Are these things your priorities?

A man was once given a glass vase, a bowl of pebbles, and a sack of large stones. He was told to put all the rocks into the glass vase. He started by filling the glass with the pebbles, but there was no room left for the stones. So he removed the pebbles, placed the large rocks in first, and then filled the gaps with the pebbles until they were all in the glass. The vase represents our lives and the capacity of time we have in a given day. We have many little "pebbles" that fill up our days: emails, deadlines, errands, favorite TV shows, or sporting events. If we aren't careful, our time can be filled with pebbles, and the big rocks are crowded out. But if we put the large stones in first—God's Word and prayer, love and obedience, investing in others—then the pebbles can fill the gaps and the big things in life won't get squeezed out.

Which "small pebble" priorities are getting in the way of your "large stone" priorities?

What do you consider the "large stone" priorities of your life?

What changes need to happen to make room for the "large stones" in your daily routine?

JESUS' UPWARD PRIORITIES

Part of following Jesus is developing the character and priorities of Jesus. The two personal studies for this week will dive into some of those priorities—both upward and outward. Carefully examine these priorities so you can replicate them in your own life. Use the passages under each priority as your guide.

First, Jesus made the Word of God a priority. Jesus saturated His heart and mind with Scriptures. At the age of 12, Jesus' parents found Him in the temple discussing Scriptures with the religious leaders. When Jesus was tempted, He resisted by quoting God's Word. Jesus often quoted and referred to Scriptural stories, never diminishing but always exalting the authority and validity of the Word.

> He answered, "It is written:
> Man must not live on bread alone
> but on every word that comes
> from the mouth of God."
> **MATTHEW 4:4**

In what ways have you used Scripture to protect yourself against temptation in the past?

> Jesus said to the Jews who had believed Him, "If you continue
> in My word, you really are My disciples. You will know the truth,
> and the truth will set you free."
> **JOHN 8:31-32**

What does Jesus instruct us to do in this passage?

How have you experienced the truth setting you free?

Second, Jesus made prayer a priority. Jesus also lived His life saturated in prayer to His Father. When you look at Jesus' life, He prayed over every major event. He prayed at His baptism. He prayed as He chose the Twelve. He prayed during busy seasons of ministry. He prayed when He was grieving. He prayed when He was hurting. His last physical act on earth was to pray from the cross. And Jesus taught His disciples to pray as well.

> Very early in the morning, while it was still dark, He got up, went out, and made His way to a deserted place. And He was praying there.
> **MARK 1:35**

> Yet He often withdrew to deserted places and prayed.
> **LUKE 5:16**

> He went out and made His way as usual to the Mount of Olives, and the disciples followed Him. When He reached the place, He told them, "Pray that you may not enter into temptation."
> **LUKE 22:39-40**

Jesus clearly had a pattern of prayer. Why do you think this was important?

Do you follow a certain pattern of prayer? If so, what is it?

We've looked at two key priorities of Jesus. As you reflect on these priorities, think of someone who you think models these priorities of Jesus.

How are these priorities lived out in a practical way in this person's life?

What can you do to implement these priorities into your life?

PERSONAL STUDY

JESUS' OUTWARD PRIORITIES

In the same way Jesus made the Word of God and prayer a priority, He also revealed upward priorities.

First, Jesus made obedience a priority. Jesus was always obedient to His Father. There was never a time when Jesus resisted or pulled aside from doing what His Father told Him to do. As a young boy, Jesus learned obedience to His parents. And as a grown man, Jesus lived a life of obedience to His Father, even when it meant suffering and death.

> 7 During His earthly life, He offered prayers and appeals with loud cries and tears to the One who was able to save Him from death, and He was heard because of His reverence. 8 Though He was God's Son, He learned obedience through what He suffered. 9 After He was perfected, He became the source of eternal salvation for all who obey Him.
> **HEBREWS 5:7-9**

What do we learn about Jesus' obedience from this passage?

> 15 "If you love Me, you will keep My commands." … 21 "The one who has My commands and keeps them is the one who loves Me. And the one who loves Me will be loved by My Father. I also will love him and will reveal Myself to him." … 23 Jesus answered, "If anyone loves Me, he will keep My word. My Father will love him, and We will come to him and make Our home with him."
> **JOHN 14:15,21,23**

How would you like to respond to Jesus' words in this passage?

What is stopping you from responding that way?

Jesus also made love a priority. Jesus loved people in a deep and profound way. Jesus loved His parents. Jesus loved His disciples. Jesus loved the outcast and oppressed. Jesus even loved those who rejected and criticized Him. Jesus spoke often about the power and priority of love and compassion. Jesus also loved the Father and exalted the Father in everything.

³⁵ And one of them, an expert in the law, asked a question to test Him: ³⁶ "Teacher, which command in the law is the greatest?" ³⁷ He said to him, "Love the Lord your God with all your heart, with all your soul, and with all your mind. ³⁸ This is the greatest and most important command. ³⁹ The second is like it: Love your neighbor as yourself. ⁴⁰ All the Law and the Prophets depend on these two commands."
MATTHEW 22:35-40

What did Jesus say about the priority of love in this passage?

⁹ God's love was revealed among us in this way: God sent His One and Only Son into the world so that we might live through Him. ¹⁰ Love consists in this: not that we loved God, but that He loved us and sent His Son to be the propitiation for our sins.
1 JOHN 4:9-10

What does Jesus' model of active love tell us about how we should love?

Finally, Jesus made investing in people a priority. Jesus drew large crowds, but His priority was training a few disciples who would change the world.

The next day He decided to leave for Galilee. Jesus found Philip and told him, "Follow Me!"
JOHN 1:43

Jesus sought out Philip and said "Follow Me!" In what other passages have you seen Jesus investing in people—making disciples that make disciples?

What one thing can you do this week to make people more of a priority in your life?

THE COST OF A DISCIPLE

Following Jesus will require sacrifice.

REFLECT

In the last session, we looked at the priorities of a disciple of Jesus. We had the opportunity to dig deeper into the priorities of Jesus and begin to apply those to our own lives. Take a few minutes to share something you learned this week or a struggle you are facing.

Use the following questions to begin the session with discussion.

Which of the assignments did you explore this week? How did it go?

What did you learn or experience while reading the Bible?

What questions would you like to ask?

PRAY

We have all experienced hardship, trials, and suffering. Today we are going to learn how to walk through those dark seasons by trusting Jesus completely. Before you dive into this session, stop and pray together as a group. Use the following guidelines as you speak with the Lord together:

- Ask God to open your heart and speak to you today.

- Seek after Him with an open heart and mind to receive what He has for you today.

- Pray for one another and for God's leadership in your lives.

INTRODUCTION

Dietrich Bonhoeffer is one of the world's foremost theologians and thinkers of the 20th century. He is most remembered for his courage to stand against the massive wave of evil that swept over his country. Bonhoeffer pastored churches in Germany during World War I and II and he saw the shifts within the German church under the pressure of the growing Nazi regime. As the German church officially supported the Aryan agenda, Bonhoeffer separated himself and led the establishment of a new "Confessing Church" that stood on the Scriptures. He left the safety of the United States to return to Germany during the most heated time in the war to join the resistance movement.

Bonhoeffer was hanged in a concentration camp in Flossenburg just after his 39th birthday, but his legacy lives on in his writings. Dietrich Bonhoeffer was a man who understood more than most the cost of discipleship that he wrote about so convincingly. He was a Christian surrounded by suffering, yet he didn't hide from it; he embraced it with devotion to God and to the people he loved. Below are some of the greatest quotes from his book *The Cost of Discipleship:*

> "To endure the cross is not tragedy; it is the suffering which is the fruit of an exclusive allegiance to Jesus Christ."[1]

> "When Christ calls a man, he bids him come and die."[2]

> "Costly grace is the treasure hidden in the field; for the sake of it a man will go and sell all that he has. It is the pearl of great price to buy which the merchant will sell all his goods. It is the kingly rule of Christ, for whose sake a man will pluck out the eye which causes him to stumble; it is the call of Jesus Christ at which the disciple leaves his nets and follows him."[3]

Which of these quotes impacts you most? Why?

What are ways we can stand for Christ in our culture today?

KNOW THE STORY

Luke 9:51 says that Jesus "set his face toward Jerusalem" (ESV). The phrase "set his face" could be translated "determined, resolute, steadfast." Jesus was focused on going up to Jerusalem. At this time He began to reveal to His disciples the death He would face there. Luke 9:22 says, "The Son of Man must suffer many things and be rejected by the elders and chief priests and scribes, and be killed, and be raised on the third day." This was the first of three clear predictions of His death, burial, and resurrection (see Matt. 16:21; Matt. 17:22-23; Matt. 20:18-19).

What awaited Jesus in Jerusalem was suffering and sacrifice. I'm sure the disciples were bewildered. They didn't fully understand what was ahead of them. Then Jesus turned to them and said these powerful words:

> 23 "If anyone wants to come with Me, he must deny himself, take up his cross daily, and follow Me. 24 For whoever wants to save his life will lose it, but whoever loses his life because of Me will save it. 25 What is a man benefited if he gains the whole world, yet loses or forfeits himself? 26 For whoever is ashamed of Me and My words, the Son of Man will be ashamed of him when He comes in His glory and that of the Father and the holy angels.
> **LUKE 9:23-26**

Why do you think Jesus is calling His disciples to endurance?

What cost have you heard about followers of Jesus having to pay?

What price do you have to pay to be a follower of Jesus?

UNPACK THE STORY

FOUR TRUTHS

So far in this study we have seen the span of two and a half years of Jesus' journey with His disciples. He first called them to "come and see" (John 1:39), to investigate His identity and His claims to be the Messiah. Then He called them to "follow Me" (Matt. 4:19), promising to make them fishers of people. He invested the next six months showing them how to fish for people and make an eternal impact. He selected twelve emerging leaders to train, so "they might be with him and he might send them out to preach" (Mark 3:14, ESV). It was at this point He revealed His power and taught them what it means to be engaged in the kingdom of God.

At the end of this training, Jesus sent them out to the towns and villages to preach and minister to the people. The Twelve apostles began to minister in Jesus' name, and God's power was on them. When they returned from their preaching tour, it was time for them to break away to rest and reflect. Jesus took them to the far north end of Israel, to a place called Caesarea Philippi. And it was there they talked about Jesus' identity as "Messiah, the Son of the living God" and His power to overcome evil (Matt. 16:16-18).

But at this point the mood changed. Jesus knew that His disciples had been fully trained. They understood His identity as the God-Man, and they were prepared to carry on the movement. Now His focus was on the cross. There are four important truths revealed in this passage:

1. We are not exempt. Many people feel that once they decide to follow Jesus they're promised a life free from trouble and trials, but that simply isn't true. Followers of Jesus face the normal hardships of life such as job loss, sickness, financial problems, pressures, and even death. All throughout Scripture we find suffering as a common and even expected occurrence in life. In 2 Timothy 2:3, Paul says: "Share in suffering as a good soldier of Christ Jesus."

What do you think Paul was trying to communicate in 2 Timothy 2:3?

---

2. We must deny ourselves. As Jesus moved toward the cross and His suffering, He called His disciples to deny themselves. "If anyone wants to come with Me, he must deny himself" (Luke 9:23). To deny yourself means to lay aside the things you desire and put Jesus first. It means to make Jesus the center of your life around which everything else revolves.

To deny yourself means to lay aside the things you desire and put Jesus first. It means to make Jesus the center of your life around which everything else revolves.

How will your lifestyle change if you deny yourself and put Jesus first?

What excuses keep you from following Jesus wholeheartedly?

3. We are to take up our cross daily. Jesus also called His disciples to sacrifice. After He told them to deny themselves He told them to take up their cross daily (see Luke 9:23). The cross was an instrument of Roman torture. It was a symbol of suffering and death. For His disciples to "take up his cross daily" meant their willingness to suffer for the name of Jesus, even if it meant death on a cross. Today Jesus calls us to follow Him, even when following Him may come at a high price.

> Whoever does not bear his own cross and come after Me cannot be My disciple.
> **LUKE 14:27**

What emotions did you experience when you read these words?

4. We are called to follow Jesus. After challenging His disciples to deny themselves and take up their cross daily, Jesus locks eyes with them and simply says, "follow Me" (Luke 9:23). Jesus is saying that a true follower endures. Even in the midst of hardship and trial, even in suffering and pain, those who are His are those who continue to follow Him.

What do you find most difficult about following Jesus in the middle of your suffering?

What is the reward for walking with Jesus through suffering?

A true follower endures. Even in the midst of hardship and trial, even in suffering and pain, those who are His are those who continue to follow Him.

ENGAGE

According to the Ethics and Religious Liberties Commission of the Southern Baptist Convention, "More Christians were martyred in the 20th century than in all previous centuries combined." According to statistics from Nigeria, India, and Iraq, it is estimated that currently more than 200 million Christians are being persecuted worldwide.

Many believers live in very dark and hostile places around the world and are extremely vulnerable to danger or even death. These believers are people like you and me. They have families, friends, and homes. They have worries and fears about the future. They want what's best for the ones they love. And they are choosing to follow Jesus in the face of great opposition.[4]

Take a moment to pray for our brothers and sisters around the world who are enduring suffering today. Ask God to give them mercy and grace to endure. Also, ask the Lord to give them boldness to share Christ in the middle of their suffering. Join with them in praying for a spiritual awakening in those closed nations.

PRAYER REQUESTS

....

....

....

....

....

....

....

....

....

....

1. Dietrich Bonhoeffer, *The Cost of Discipleship* (New York: SCM Press, Ltd., 1959), 88.
2. Ibid, 11.
3. Ibid, 45.
4. "Christian Persecution: Quick Facts: Reliable and Informative Snapshots of the Focus Issue," The Ethics and Religious Liberty Commission. Available at: erlc.com.

In addition to studying God's Word, work with your group leader to create a plan for personal study, worship, and application between now and the next session. Select from the following optional activities to match your personal preferences and available time.

⬆ Worship

☑ Read your Bible. Complete the reading plan on page 72.

☐ Connect with God by engaging the devotional on page 73.

☐ Sometimes the greatest worship we offer the Lord is through our brokenness. Take time to be alone with the Lord this week. Read the story of a woman who worshiped Jesus through her brokenness—Luke 7:36-50. Cast your cares on Him—your worries, fears, dreams, pain, disappointments, and shame. Praise Jesus and anoint Him with your worship.

➡ ⬅ Personal Study

☐ Read and interact with "Four Truths" on page 74.

☐ Read and interact with "Put It Into Practice" on page 76.

⬅ ➡ Application

☐ Connect with others. Intentionally look around you for people who are hurting. Ask God to give you His eyes of compassion to see hurting people in your family, office, neighborhood, or school. Do something this week to demonstrate love and compassion to that hurting person. As you love him or her, Christ is loving that person through you.

☐ Memorize Luke 9:23: "If anyone would come with Me, he must deny himself, take up his cross daily, and follow Me."

☐ Write an email this week and send it to someone who is going through a trial. Include in your email words of encouragement and promises from God's Word. Share how the Lord has carried you through a trial in your life.

☐ Other:

WORSHIP

READING PLAN

Read through the following Scripture passages this week. Use the space provided to record your thoughts and responses.

Day 1
Matthew 10:16-39

Day 2
Matthew 24:1-27

Day 3
Luke 14:25-35

Day 4
John 16:1-33

Day 5
Philippians 1:12-30

Day 6
Philippians 3:1-21

Day 7
2 Timothy 3:1-17

NO TURNING BACK

In the 1800s, a revival movement exploded across India. Hundreds of missionaries from Europe, Australia, and the United States flooded into the country, especially in the once closed territory of northern India. While resistance to the gospel was at times hostile and many missionaries were martyred for their faith, the gospel continued to spread rapidly. A Welsh missionary who had endured many persecutions for his faith led a family to Christ in the province of Assam. The tribal leaders decided to make an example of this family, forcing them to recant or be executed. Witnesses reported that when asked to recant or see his children murdered, the man simply replied, "I have decided to follow Jesus, and there is no turning back."

After the death of his children he reportedly said, "The world can be behind me, but the cross is still before me." And after seeing his wife shot with arrows, the man declared, "Though no one is here to go with me, still I will follow Jesus." After this statement of faith, the man joined his family in heaven.

The story of this man's courage spread rapidly and his entire village came to Christ, including those who carried out the senseless murders. Word of this man and the revival reached a famous Indian evangelist, Sadhu Singh who put these dying words into a song that was sung all through the churches in India. This song was sung at many Billy Graham crusades and had a profound effect on thousands upon thousands of people. Reflect on the words of this song. Have you decided to follow Jesus no matter what?

> I have decided to follow Jesus;
> No turning back, no turning back.[1]

If you haven't heard this song or want to be reminded of it's biblically-rooted lyrics, take a moment to search for the lyrics in their entirety on www.hymnary.org. Listen to the song or read over the words and ponder the hymn's rich meaning. This is a great way to worship Jesus and thank Him for all He has done for us.

Take the time now to find a verse from Scripture or a line from a biblically-rooted song and write it down below. Spend time meditating on those words, and speak them aloud in a prayer to God.

---

1. John Clark, "I Have Decided to Follow Jesus," *The Baptist Hymnal* (Nashville, TN: Convention Press, 1991), 305.

FOUR TRUTHS

Go even deeper into the text this week as you study four primary truths found in Luke 9:23-26. Reread the passage and the "Unpack the Story" section to familiarize yourself with the text.

1. We are not exempt. Trials are part of life. They come to Christians and non-Christians alike. But in Christ we approach trials differently. Instead of being shocked or caught off guard by trials, we anticipate them, knowing that through Christ we can overcome any trial we face (see Rom. 8:37). In fact, as we see trials in our lives from God's perspective, we realize that every problem we face is another opportunity to trust God and mature as a follower of Jesus. Through them, God is producing in us patience, endurance, strength, character, hope, and faith. Just as weights in a gym break down muscles only to make them stronger, the struggles of life serve to make us stronger as we put our whole weight down on God's promises and trust Jesus to carry us through.

> ³ Not only that, but we also rejoice in our afflictions, because we know that affliction produces endurance, ⁴ endurance produces proven character, and proven character produces hope. ⁵ This hope will not disappoint us, because God's love has been poured out in our hearts through the Holy Spirit who was given to us.
> **ROMANS 5:3-5**

What do these verses tell us about the trials God allows to come into the life of every believer?

2. We must deny ourselves. Denying ourselves is a call to godly and holy living. When we deny our natural desire to sin in order to please God, then we are living a life that honors Christ.

Jesus encountered three men who wanted to follow Him, but each man had an excuse. Read this account in Luke 9:57-62 and answer the following questions.

In what way was each man unwilling to deny himself and follow Jesus?

What areas of your life would have to be put away for you to follow Jesus completely?

3. We are to take up our cross daily. Karen Watson was a missionary in Iraq. She was killed with four other missionaries on March 15, 2004. This is a portion of a letter she sent home to be read on her death.

> Dear Pastor Phil and Pastor Roger,
>
> You should only be opening this letter in the event of my death. When God calls there are no regrets. I tried to share my heart with you as much as possible, my heart for the Nations. I wasn't called to a place. I was called to Him. To obey was my objective, to suffer was expected, His glory was my reward, His glory is my reward. … I was called not to comfort or success but to obedience. Some of my favorite Scriptures are: Isaiah 6, you know the one. Second Corinthians 5:15-21, 1 Peter 1:3, Colossians 4:2-6, Romans 15:20, Psalms 25 and 27. You can look through my Scofield and see where it is marked. Please use only what you want or feel best. There is no joy outside of knowing Jesus and serving Him. I love you two and my church family.
>
> In His care, Salaam,
> Karen[1]

In what ways does Karen's example challenge you?

4. We are called to follow Jesus. Consider the benefits of following Christ in the midst of trial.

> [2] Consider it a great joy, my brothers, whenever you experience various trials, [3] knowing that the testing of your faith produces endurance. [4] But endurance must do its complete work, so that you may be mature and complete, lacking nothing.
> **JAMES 1:2-4**

Think of a person you know who has walked through suffering and hardship and continued to follow Jesus. What does his or her story teach you concerning what to do when persecuted?

1. As quoted in Andy Cook, "Sermon: Fine-tune Your Focus: 2 Corinthians 4." June 29, 2007. Available at lifeway.com. Accessed May 1, 2015.

PUT IT INTO PRACTICE

We have already seen that part of following Jesus is self-denial. Most of our time is taken up satisfying ourselves as quickly as possible with the things we want. In what ways have you practiced self-denial lately?

Think about ways you can deny yourself and exalt Jesus. Maybe you could deny your urge to be first and let someone else go ahead of you. You might deny the urge to eat and use your lunch break to fast and pray. You could even deny the urge to entertain yourself. Instead of watching TV or going to a movie, spend time visiting someone in the hospital.

Ask God to show you the areas in your life where He wants you to practice self-denial, and then record your thoughts in response to the following questions.

What message does our culture send about personal happiness?

How does this influence your thinking or distract you from denying yourself and exalting God?

What are your hardest urges to deny? How have you overcome these urges in the past?

List five practical ways you can demonstrate self-denial to others. These may be people you're close to or people you've never met before.

As you have worked through this session, you may be walking through a season of hardship and trial in your own life. During these times it's important to draw close to the Lord and lean wholly on His promises and presence. Below are some promises God gives to those going through trials. Study each one and write down the promise. Which stands out to you? Who can you share these promises with this week?

Psalm 34:18

Isaiah 43:1-2

1 Corinthians 10:13

2 Corinthians 1:3-4

2 Corinthians 12:8-9

Hebrews 13:5

James 1:12

SESSION 6

THE FRUIT
OF A DISCIPLE

A follower of Jesus makes disciples
who make disciples.

REFLECT

Last session explored the cost of following Jesus. We saw that the Bible has a lot to say about suffering and how we face trials and hardships as followers of Jesus. We also had an opportunity to discover God's incredible promises for those who are walking through trials and suffering. Today we are going to look at the incredible privilege we have of joining Jesus in His global cause to make disciples who make disciples. If you ever wondered how God could use you in a powerful way to make a difference in this world, you are about to find out!

Use the following questions to begin the session with discussion.

Which of the assignments did you explore this week? How did it go?

What did you learn or experience while reading the Bible?

What questions would you like to ask?

PRAY

Before you dive into this session, stop and pray together as a group. Use the following guidelines as you speak with the Lord together:

- Seek after Him with an open heart and mind to receive what He has for you today.

- Pray for one another and for God to speak to each of you.

- Ask God to open up your heart and mind to His plan for your life.

INTRODUCTION

Would you rather have a penny a day doubled every day for a month or a million dollars in cash? Most people would probably grab the million without even questioning it. But you might be surprised at how quickly pennies can pile up!

Day 1	$0.01	Day 11	$10.24	Day 21	$10,485.76
Day 2	$0.02	Day 12	$20.48	Day 22	$20,971.52
Day 3	$0.04	Day 13	$40.96	Day 23	$41,943.04
Day 4	$0.08	Day 14	$81.92	Day 24	$83,886.08
Day 5	$0.16	Day 15	$163.84	Day 25	$167,772.16
Day 6	$0.32	Day 16	$327.68	Day 26	$335,544.32
Day 7	$0.64	Day 17	$655.36	Day 27	$671,088.64
Day 8	$1.28	Day 18	$1,310.72	Day 28	$1,342,177.28
Day 9	$2.56	Day 19	$2,621.44	Day 29	$2,684,354.56
Day 10	$5.12	Day 20	$5,242.88	Day 30	$5,368,709.12

By the end of one month, one penny has exploded to more than 5 million dollars. That's five times the million dollars originally offered! Why is it so much more? Multiplication. By doubling your pennies every day, you unleash a tidal wave of multiplication. Every banker and business leader understands the power of multiplication. Every hedge fund investor or financial planner understands the power of multiplication. And Jesus understood the power of multiplication, too.

Jesus trained His disciples to make disciples who would make disciples. Within 2 years, His twelve disciples filled Jerusalem with their teaching (see Acts 5:28). In 4 years, the churches were multiplying and growing throughout all Judea, Samaria, and Galilee (see Acts 9:31). Within 19 years, they "turned the world upside down" (Acts 17:6). And within 30 years, the gospel was bearing fruit and growing around the world (see Col. 1:6). Jesus' disciples unleashed a movement of multiplication that continues even today to sweep around the globe and reach every people group on the planet.

Why do you think the early disciples multiplied so rapidly?

What keeps believers and churches from multiplying today?

KNOW THE STORY

In a darkened room, with only a candle to light the table, Jesus gathered His disciples for one last meal and spoke plainly about His coming betrayal and death. These were Jesus' final words to the disciples in whom He had invested three and a half years of His life. After the meal, He led them out from the upper room, down the stone streets of Jerusalem, out the gate, across the Kidron Valley, and up the Mount of Olives. Along the way, they passed through a moonlit vineyard. Cradling a cluster of ripe grapes in His hands, Jesus spoke to them about how their lives could be used to create a movement that would change the world.

¹ I am the true vine, and My Father is the vineyard keeper. ² Every branch in Me that does not produce fruit He removes, and He prunes every branch that produces fruit so that it will produce more fruit. ³ You are already clean because of the word I have spoken to you. ⁴ Remain in Me, and I in you. Just as a branch is unable to produce fruit by itself unless it remains on the vine, so neither can you unless you remain in Me. ⁵ I am the vine; you are the branches. The one who remains in Me and I in him produces much fruit, because you can do nothing without Me. ⁶ If anyone does not remain in Me, he is thrown aside like a branch and he withers. They gather them, throw them into the fire, and they are burned. ⁷ If you remain in Me and My words remain in you, ask whatever you want and it will be done for you. ⁸ My Father is glorified by this: that you produce much fruit and prove to be My disciples.

¹⁶ You did not choose Me, but I chose you. I appointed you that you should go out and produce fruit and that your fruit should remain, so that whatever you ask the Father in My name, He will give you.
JOHN 15:1-8,16

What does it mean to produce fruit as a disciple of Jesus?

How do you respond to Jesus' words in verse 16?

UNPACK THE STORY

MEASURING FRUITFULNESS

Jesus is teaching an important principle here about fruitfulness. When a person chooses to follow Jesus, God expects that person to begin to bear fruit that brings Him glory and proves to people watching that he or she truly belongs to Jesus. You may be asking, "What is spiritual fruit?" Look up the following verses to find the three ways fruitfulness can be measured in a believer's life.

Galatians 5:22-23
Spiritual fruit is measured by _____.

Philippians 1:11
Spiritual fruit is measured by _____.

Romans 1:13
Spiritual fruit is measured by _____.

Jesus is teaching an important principle here about fruitfulness. When a person chooses to follow Jesus, God expects that person to begin to bear fruit that brings Him glory and proves to people watching that he or she truly belongs to Jesus.

1. Character fruit. Galatians 5:22-23 describes character fruit this way: love, joy, peace, patience, kindness, faith, gentleness, and self-control. When a person receives Christ by faith, the Spirit of God comes to live inside that person (see Eph. 1:13-14; 1 Cor. 6:19-20; Rom. 8:9). The Spirit goes to work transforming that person into the likeness of Jesus from the inside out. The longer you walk with Christ, the more you are transformed by the Spirit to look more and more like Him.

> We all, with unveiled faces, are looking as in a mirror at the glory of the Lord and are being transformed into the same image from glory to glory; this is from the Lord who is the Spirit.
> **2 CORINTHIANS 3:18**

2. Conduct fruit. Another fruit in the life of every Christ-follower is conduct fruit. In Philippians 1:11, the apostle Paul speaks about the "fruit of righteousness." This is the fruit of a life that lives righteously and serves God faithfully.

Followers of Jesus are called to be different from everyone else. Followers of Jesus produce good works (see Eph. 2:10; Titus 3:14) that glorify God and demonstrate His love to the world (see Matt. 5:16). So when you love God and love people, choose integrity and honesty, lead with compassion, serve with humility, and give generously, you are reflecting Jesus to the people around you.

3. Conversion fruit. The final fruit in the life of a follower of Jesus is conversion fruit. The apostle Paul, in writing to the Romans, looked forward to a "fruitful ministry" when he arrived in Rome (see Rom. 1:13). He saw the salvation of many people like a huge reaping harvest at the end of a long season. Jesus often used the same analogy. He spoke of people coming to faith as the reaping of a spiritual harvest. Jesus said, "The harvest is abundant, but the workers are few" (Matt. 9:37; see also Luke 10:2; John 4:35-38).

When you share the gospel with a person far from God and they come to faith in Jesus, you are bearing spiritual fruit (see Prov. 11:30). When you invest in a person—just as Jesus invested in His disciples—and you teach him or her to walk with God and invest in others, you are producing lasting spiritual fruit.

Which area do you think needs the most attention in your life?

In which area are you seeing growth?

Who are you looking forward to investing in spiritually?

When you invest in a person—just as Jesus invested in His disciples—and you teach him or her to walk with God and invest in others, you are producing lasting spiritual fruit.

ENGAGE

In John 15 Jesus teaches us about bearing spiritual fruit. While Jesus could have been talking about character fruit or conduct fruit, most likely Jesus had conversion fruit in mind. He was casting a vision of what a fruitful life that makes disciples who make disciples looks like. This was the last time Jesus spoke to His disciples before His crucifixion and resurrection. For three and a half years He poured His life into them, teaching them how to preach the gospel, minister to the hurting, and make disciples who make disciples. The original twelve were now becoming more and more like Jesus.

Now the Twelve had multiplied into 70 disciple makers (see Luke 10:1). They were already beginning to multiply! Jesus envisioned a day when His disciples would multiply, making disciples who would make disciples, and their influence would change the world. But on this night He used a simple object lesson of a vine, a branch, and some fruit to demonstrate His desire for them to multiply.

What things do you need to work on to live a more fruitful life?

Share some action steps you plan to take this week.

Disciple making is a decision. No one will make you invest in others. It's a choice you make based on the command of Jesus (see Matt. 28:18-20). To get started, ask the Lord to give you the names of a few people you can invest in. Write the names below. As a group, pray over these names and how God will use you to share the fruit that God has brought to your life.

Names of people you plan to invest in:

PRAYER REQUESTS

....

....

....

....

....

....

In addition to studying God's Word, work with your group leader to create a plan for personal study, worship, and application between now and the next session. Select from the following optional activities to match your personal preferences and available time.

⬆ Worship

☑ Read your Bible. Complete the reading plan on page 86.

☐ Connect with God by engaging the devotional on page 87.

☐ Read 1 Corinthians 3:10-15 and 1 Thessalonians 2:19. What is Paul's source of joy when he stands before the Lord? Evaluate the way you spend your time, talents, resources, and relationships. Spend time before the Lord praising Him for His grace in your life.

➡ ⬅ Personal Study

☐ Read and interact with "Stages of Fruitfulness" on page 88

☐ Read and interact with "The Fruitful Life" on page 90.

⬅ ➡ Application

☐ Connect with others. Take someone out to lunch this week who doesn't know Jesus. Find out about him or her—background, struggles, stressors. Make it your goal in the next 30 days to begin to encourage this person in one area of his or her life. All the while, pray for an opportunity to share what Jesus has done for you.

☐ Memorize John 15:8: "My Father is glorified by this: that you produce much fruit and prove to be My disciples."

☐ Spend time journaling. In 2 Timothy 2:2 Paul mentions a four-generation movement of multiplication: Paul, Timothy, faithful men, and others. Once a person makes disciples to the fourth generation, a movement is born. Journal your own personal movement of multiplication. Who is your Paul (someone who has discipled you or invested in your life)? Who are your "faithful men" (those you could personally disciple)? Who are the "others" that your disciples could train?

☐ Other:

 **WORSHIP**

READING PLAN

Read through the following Scripture passages this week. Use the space provided to record your thoughts and responses.

Day 1
Luke 6:27-49

Day 2
John 13:1-20

Day 3
Romans 15:1-21

Day 4
1 Corinthians 12:1-31

Day 5
Ephesians 5:1-21

Day 6
Philippians 2:1-18

Day 7
1 John 5:1-21

LASTING FRUIT

Mount Arbel is the highest point along the Sea of Galilee. On a clear day, from Mount Arbel you can see Mount Hermon that borders Syria, the Golan Heights that border Syria and Jordan, and Mount Carmel that borders Lebanon. You can also see the Via Maris (Way of the Sea) which was the popular trade route in Jesus' day that ran through Galilee and led travelers to the most powerful nations of the Middle East. From Mount Arbel you can see the world.

It's possible that it was here Jesus met His disciples one more time. The last time He had spoken to them about creating a movement of multiplication, they were together in the moonlit vineyard the night before He was arrested. At that time He spoke to them about vines, branches, and fruit. But this time, He stood in broad daylight with His disciples in His resurrected body and looked at the nations. And He spoke to them words that would change them forever!

> Go, therefore, and make disciples of all nations, baptizing them in the name of the Father and of the Son and of the Holy Spirit, teaching them to observe everything I have commanded you. And remember, I am with you always, to the end of the age.
> **MATTHEW 28:19-20**

They had been trained. They knew how to lead people to Christ, and they knew how to invest in a few. And in a few days, Jesus would send the Spirit to empower them to ignite a movement that would change the world (Acts 2:1-41). They had everything they needed, but they still had to choose. They had to choose to follow Jesus, to live as He lived, and to walk as He walked.

The same thing could be said about us. We have the same Spirit they had. We have the same Word of God they had. We have the same command they had—"Go and make disciples." The question remains, will we follow Jesus? The world is waiting for men and women who will dare to follow Jesus and join Him in His global cause to make disciples of all nations.

There is no greater joy or thrill, no greater reward or satisfaction, than joining Jesus in the greatest cause on earth! And when your life is over, you'll have lasting fruit to show for your life. Fruit that will remain forever!

What is your reaction to this passage in Matthew 28?

How will you join Jesus in His global cause to make disciples of all nations?

STAGES OF FRUITFULNESS

Take a moment to read John 15:1-8,16 again. As you read this passage, notice that Jesus refers to different stages of fruitfulness. See if you can identify them.

No Fruit: There are those who have no fruit (v. 1). These are the people who know Christ but have never invested in anyone spiritually. They have never trained anyone how to walk with God. Jesus said, "Every branch in me that does not bear fruit he takes away" (John 15:2, ESV). The phrase "takes away" literally means to "lift up, or to move somewhere else." Some translate it "to cut off." The idea is a branch that has fallen off the trellis and is in the mud. It's dirty; it can't get sunlight; and it can't get air, so it is barren.

There are many Christians like that. They have fallen into some area of sin or disobedience. They have become entangled in a quagmire of habits and behaviors that have grieved God's Spirit (see Eph. 4:30), and consequently they have nothing to show for their walk with Christ. But here's the good news: Even if you have fallen and you aren't bearing fruit for Christ, Jesus can change that. The move from "no fruit" to "some fruit" requires repentance. Jesus said to a church that had become apathetic and barren, "Consider how far you have fallen! Repent and do the things you did at first" (Rev. 2:5, NIV).

Repentance means acknowledging that you've wandered from God and making a u-turn back to Him. First John 1:9 gives us a tremendous promise: "If we confess our sins, He is faithful and righteous to forgive us our sins and to cleanse us from all unrighteousness.." If you turn to Jesus and ask Him to forgive and restore you, He will. He will lift you up, clean you off, and restore you to fruitfulness.

Some Fruit: There are also people who are bearing some fruit for Jesus, but they could do much more. "Every branch in Me that does not produce fruit He removes, and He prunes every branch that produces fruit so that it will produce more fruit" (John 15:2). This is the person who is sharing his faith and investing in people sometimes—but only when it's convenient. He is serving God occasionally. He could be doing so much more for God's kingdom. Jesus said that this person is unfruitful because he's distracted. Many times people say, "I wish I could really serve God, but I'm so busy." The pace of our lives and the demands of our days often choke out our fruitfulness for God. Jesus put it this way: "All too quickly the message is crowded out by the worries of this life, the lure of wealth, and the desire for other things, so no fruit is produced" (Mark 4:19, NLT). Is this you? Do you find that the busyness of life, the desire for more things, or stress and anxiety rob you of being really fruitful for God?

The move from "some fruit" to "more fruit" requires pruning. Just like a master gardener prunes branches so that a plant can produce more fruit, for our lives to become more fruitful we must be pruned. That may simply mean that you need to prune your schedule. It may require you to thin out your responsibilities to make more time to serve God and invest in others. But in this story, Jesus said the Father is the one doing the pruning. And there are times when God uses trials, hardships, and challenges to prune away the things we hold onto in this life so that we can be fully reliant on Him. Hebrews 12:11 says, "No discipline seems enjoyable at the time, but painful. Later on, however, it yields the fruit of peace and righteousness to those who have been trained by it." While pruning is painful, if you hold fast to Jesus, you will find that on the other side of the pruning is incredible fruitfulness.

Much Fruit: Finally, Jesus mentions some who are producing more fruit, but they have potential to produce "much fruit" (John 15:5). This is the person who has come through a season of pruning and God is producing fruitfulness. They are seeing people come to Christ; they are investing in people spiritually; and God is at work. But there is still more that God wants to do through this person. He wants to use him or her to produce "much fruit"—fruit that is overflowing and overabundant.

Picture baskets and baskets of fruit. Then picture a huge harvest of people who are touched and transformed by God through this person's life. That is what Jesus has in mind for every one of us. But the move from "more fruit" to "much fruit" requires abiding. Jesus said, "I am the vine; you are the branches. Whoever abides in Me and I in him, he it is that bears much fruit, for apart from me you can do nothing" (John 15:5, ESV). Jesus uses the word "abide" eight times in these few verses. The word means "to stay, to dwell, to continue, to make your home with." For a person to be used by God to his or her ultimate potential, it requires abiding with Jesus. It means that you draw close to Him; you spend time in prayer and His Word; you learn what it means to know Him deeply and personally; and you completely rely on His power and strength day by day. Just as branches have to stay vitally connected to the vine so that the life and power to produce fruit can pass through them, we must stay vitally connected with Jesus so that His life and power can work through us to produce fruit that will last for eternity.

Just like a branch that is cut off from the vine eventually withers up and loses its usefulness, when anyone pulls back from Jesus, they fall short of their full redemptive potential. You will never produce much fruit in your own effort. Redemptive fruit only comes by yielding your life to Jesus and asking Him to do in you and through you what only He can do!

What stage of fruitfulness are you in right now?

What do you need to do to move to the next stage of fruitfulness?

What will it cost you to produce "much fruit" for Jesus?

THE FRUITFUL LIFE

You may be thinking, *I want my life to make a difference. I want to bear fruit that will last for eternity, but I'm not sure how to do that.* First John 2:6 says, "Whoever claims to live in him must live as Jesus did" (NIV). Jesus is our model for fruitful living, so living a fruitful life is really living a life that models the life of Jesus. Let's get practical here for a minute. If you want to live a fruitful life by making disciples who make disciples, there are three simple things Jesus did that you need to do.

1. Walk with God. Jesus lived in close fellowship and prayerful dependence on His Father. He spent time in prayer with His Father (see Mark 1:35). Jesus lived in complete reliance on His Father (John 5:19,30). If you want to live the fruitful life, it begins by drawing close to Jesus. Jesus put it this way, "Abide in me" (John 15:4, ESV). This means that every day you're seeking to draw close to Jesus by saturating your life with prayer and God's Word, drawing up nourishment for Him and allowing Him to speak to you and lead you. It also means that you place Jesus first in your life (see Matt. 6:33) and live to please Him (see 2 Cor. 5:9,15). Over the three and half years of Jesus' ministry, He was teaching His disciples to love Him and rely on Him for everything. Then when He left He promised He would not leave them alone, but He would send another counselor just like Himself, His Spirit, to be with them forever (see John 14:15-18). As you walk in step with the Spirit, He will guide you and lead you to real fruitfulness (see Gal. 5:16,25).

Set a regular time daily to meet with God. Establish a plan to read God's Word every day and seek His face. Get involved in a local church and make worshiping and serving God a priority.

What does it mean to walk with God?

Jesus taught that walking with God is more about loving Him, relying on Him, and abiding in Him for everything rather than asking, "What can I do for God today?" Do you struggle with this thinking? Why or why not?

2. Reach the lost. Jesus pursued people who were far from God. In fact, Jesus said His purpose for coming was "to seek and to save the lost" (Luke 19:10). Jesus loved people. He knew that people mattered to the Father and they mattered to Him, too. He went out of His way to strike up spiritual conversations with all kinds of people. Later, Jesus said to His disciples, "As the Father has sent Me, I also send you" (John 20:21). Jesus spent three and half years training the disciples to actively share the gospel with people who had yet to say yes to Jesus. They became passionate sharers of the gospel, and many people came to Christ as a result of their courage. As you are walking with God, begin to pursue people in your life who don't know Christ. You can begin by writing down the names of four or five people who don't know Jesus. Start praying for them daily. Engage them in conversation. Invite them out to eat and find out what's going on in their lives. Begin to care for their needs and share with them how Jesus has changed your life. You may want to invite them to church with you. As the Spirit leads, share with them how they can come to know Jesus personally. The apostle Paul said, "For I am not ashamed of the gospel, because it is God's power for salvation to everyone who believes, first to the Jew, and also to the Greek" (Rom. 1:16).

Think of someone in your life who models boldness when it comes to sharing his or her faith. What attributes enable this person to speak so boldly for Christ?

3. Invest in a few. When you look at the life of Jesus, He made it a priority to invest in a few people for maximum impact. The majority of Jesus' ministry was not spent preaching to the crowds, but investing in a few. He taught them to love God. He taught them how to pray and read God's Word. He taught them how to share the gospel and stand strong under trials. He taught them how to make disciples who would make disciples and eventually change the course of history. The vision Jesus had for His disciples is the vision He has for your life. In many ways, your life is like a stone thrown into a still lake. It makes a splash for a moment, but then it quickly disappears. It leaves behind ripples that continue to go on until they reach the shore. When you invest your life in a few people and train them to do the same, you're creating ripples that continue long after you're gone! God wants to use you to create a movement of multiplication that will continue to reach people and invest in people long after you leave this world. That happens as you disciple one life at a time. Ask God to give you one person every six months to disciple. Take this book you just completed and walk someone else through it. Then, challenge them to do the same. Making disciples is how we glorify God and how we fulfill the purpose Jesus has for our lives!

What action steps will you take this week to invest in someone's life? Be specific.

DISCIPLESPATH

If your group is continuing on the *Disciples Path* journey, choose your next study using the chart below or find other discipleship studies at www.lifeway.com/goadults.

THE BEGINNING
First Steps for New Disciples

THE WAY
Discovering Christ's
Path of Discipleship

THE CALL
Counting the Cost
of Following Christ

THE MISSION
Joining God in His Work

DISCIPLESPATH

THE TRUTH
Engaging the Foundations
of the Faith

THE LIFE
Living the Spiritual Disciplines

TAKE THE NEXT STEP.

Disciples Path is a series of resources founded on Jesus' model of discipleship. Created by experienced disciple makers across the nation, it is an intentional path of transformational discipleship. While most small-group studies facilitate transformation through relationship and information, these disciple-making resources do it through the principles of modeling, practicing, and multiplying.

- Leaders model a biblical life.
- Disciples follow and practice from the leader.
- Disciples become disciple makers and multiply through *Disciples Path.*

Each of the six studies in the *Disciples Path* series has been written and approved by disciple makers for one-on-one settings as well as small groups. The series includes:

1. THE BEGINNING
Take the first step for a new believer and new disciple.

2. THE WAY
Walk through the Gospels and follow the journey of Jesus and the first disciples.

3. THE CALL
Gain a deeper understanding of what it means to follow Christ in everyday life.

4. THE TRUTH
Dive into the doctrinal truths of biblical discipleship.

5. THE LIFE
Take a deeper look at the essential disciplines and practices of following Christ.

6. THE MISSION
Get equipped for God's mission and discover your role in joining Him in the world.

To learn more or take the next step, visit lifeway.com/disciplespath.

LEADER INSTRUCTIONS

As a group leader or mentor, you have a vital role in the process of discipleship—one that involves both blessing and responsibility. Keep in mind the following guidelines as you faithfully obey the Great Commission.

YOUR GOAL

Remember that your ultimate goal in the discipleship process is spiritual transformation. The best fruit for your efforts as a leader is spiritual growth that results in transformed hearts—both for you and for the disciples under your care.

Remember also that spiritual transformation is most likely to occur when a godly leader applies truth to the heart of a person while that person is in a teachable posture. As the leader, you have direct control over the first two of those conditions; you can also encourage and support disciples as they seek a teachable posture. Take advantage of those opportunities.

YOUR METHODS

Use the following suggestions as you work toward the goal of spiritual transformation.

- **Pray daily.** Studies have shown that leaders who pray every day for the disciples under their care see the most spiritual fruit during the discipleship process. Your ultimate goal is spiritual transformation; therefore, seek the Holy Spirit.

- **Teach information.** This resource contains helpful information on the basic elements of the Christian faith. During group discussions, you'll want to be familiar enough with the content to avoid reading each page verbatim. Highlighting key words or even creating your own bullet points will help you facilitate the time most effectively. Prepare in advance.

- **Seek conversation.** As you lead disciples through the material, seek to engage them in meaningful conversation. To help you, discussion questions have been provided throughout the group portion of each session. These questions provide an opportunity to pause and allow each disciple to react to the teaching. They also allow you as the disciple maker an opportunity to gauge how each person is progressing along the path of discipleship.

- **Model practices.** Many disciples learn best by observing others. Therefore, each session of this resource includes opportunities for you to model the attributes, disciplines, and practices of a growing disciple of Jesus. Take advantage of these opportunities by intentionally showing disciples how to pray, interact with God's Word, worship God, and so on—and by inviting feedback and questions.

May God bless your efforts to guide others toward the blessing of new life through Christ and continued transformation through His Spirit.

NOTES

Group Directory

Name: _____   Name: _____

Home phone: _____   Home phone: _____

Mobile phone: _____   Mobile phone: _____

Email: _____   Email: _____

Social media: _____   Social media: _____

Name: _____   Name: _____

Home phone: _____   Home phone: _____

Mobile phone: _____   Mobile phone: _____

Email: _____   Email: _____

Social media: _____   Social media: _____

Name: _____   Name: _____

Home phone: _____   Home phone: _____

Mobile phone: _____   Mobile phone: _____

Email: _____   Email: _____

Social media: _____   Social media: _____

Name: _____   Name: _____

Home phone: _____   Home phone: _____

Mobile phone: _____   Mobile phone: _____

Email: _____   Email: _____

Social media: _____   Social media: _____

Name: _____   Name: _____

Home phone: _____   Home phone: _____

Mobile phone: _____   Mobile phone: _____

Email: _____   Email: _____

Social media: _____   Social media: _____